NOW THAT BABY IS HOME

T0328049

NOW THAT BABY IS HOME

William Sears, M.D.
&
Martha Sears, R.N.

Published in association with the literary agency of Alive Communications, 1465 Kelly Johnson Blvd., Suite #320, Colorado Springs, CO 80920.

Published in Nashville, Tennessee, by Thomas Nelson, Inc.

The Bible version used in this publication is THE NEW KING JAMES VERSION. Copyright © 1979, 1980, 1982, 1990, Thomas Nelson, Inc., Publishers.

Library of Congress Cataloging-in-Publication Data

Sears, William, M.D.
    Now that baby is home / William Sears and
Martha Sears.
        p.   cm.—(The Sears parenting library)
    "Janet Thoma books."
    Updated ed. of: Christian parenting and child care.
1991.
    Includes bibliographical references (p. 237) and index.
    ISBN 0-7852-7207-0 (pbk.)
    1. Family—Religious life.   2. Infants—Care.
3. Parenting—Religious aspects—Christianity.
I. Sears, Martha.   II. Sears, William, M.D. Christian
parenting and child care.   III. Title.   IV. Series:
Sears, William, M.D. Sears parenting library.
BV4526.2.S437   1998
248.8'45—dc21   97–47385
                                                        CIP

Printed in the United States of America
1 2 3 4 5 6 7 — 04 03 02 01 00 99 98

Contents

Preface

My dear Christian parents, this book arose out of my own deep love and concern for children as one of God's greatest gifts to us. A child is a gift for us to love, to nurture, and ultimately to return to Him a finished person.

Because they are such a precious gift, I feel that our Creator has given us a divine design for the care and feeding of His children. Over the past decade and a half, I have been increasingly concerned that this design is not being followed. As a result, parents are having difficulty training their children, who are departing from the way they should go. In The Sears Parenting Library I want to convey what I believe is God's design for parenting, and I will offer practical suggestions on how to follow that design.

During my past twenty years in pediatric practice I have carefully observed what parenting styles work for most parents most of the time. Besides learning from my patients, I have been blessed with a wonderful wife, Martha, who is a professional mother. If, after reading this book, you are more able to achieve the three goals of parenting, which are to know your child, to help your child feel right, and to lead your child to Christ, then I will have served my Lord in writing this book.

William P. Sears, M.D.
San Clemente, California

Introduction

The main purpose of *So You're Going to Be a Parent* is to help parents achieve what I believe are the three primary goals of Christian parenting:

1. To know your child
2. To help your child feel right
3. To lead your child to Christ

Each child comes wired with a unique set of characteristics called *temperament*. No two children come wired the same. Each child also has a certain level of needs that, if met, will enable him to reach his fullest potential. Some children have higher needs than others.

Each parent is endowed with a natural ability to nurture. Some children require more nurturing than others, and some parents have a higher level of giving than others. Implied in the concept of a loving Creator is that God would not give to parents a child they could not handle. God's matching program is perfect; His law of supply and demand will work if people practice a style of parenting that allows the divine design for the parent-child relationship to develop.

The term *parenting style* means "a way of caring for your child." Restrained parenting is one parenting style that is earmarked by phrases like, "Let your baby try it out," "What, you're still nursing?" "Don't let him sleep with you," "Get him on a schedule," "You're making him too dependent," and "You're going to spoil her." These common admonitions from trusted advisers to vulnerable new parents keep them from fully enjoying their child.

The style of parenting I believe God designed for the care and feeding of His children is what I call "attachment parenting," which encourages new parents to respond to their child's cues without restraint. The fundamentals of attachment parenting include the eight baby Bs:

1. *Bonding*. Pray for your preborn baby during pregnancy. Also, unless a medical complication prevents it, keep your newborn in touch with you continuously, or at least as many hours a day as possible during the early weeks. Familiarity builds your confidence because it allows you to get to know your baby intimately.

2. *Breastfeeding*. This is an exercise in babyreading, helping you learn to read your baby's cues. Breastfeeding also stimulates an outpouring of the hormones prolactin and oxytocin. These mothering hormones act like biochemical helpers, which may also be the biological basis of God's design for the term *mother's intuition*.

3. *Babywearing*. Closeness promotes familiarity. Wear your baby in a babysling as many hours a day as you and your baby enjoy. Because baby is so close to you in your arms and in contact with you, you get to know your baby better. And your baby is calmer and easier to care for.

4. *Bedsharing*. Truly, there is no one right place for baby to sleep. Wherever all family members get the best sleep is the right arrangement for them, and that arrangement may vary at different stages of baby's development. Allowing baby to sleep next to you in your bed, especially in the early months, is valuable for busy parents who do not have much daytime contact with their baby. Bedsharing allows you to reconnect with your baby at night to make up for being out of touch during the day.

5. *Believe in baby's cries*. A baby's cry is a baby's language. It is designed for the survival of the baby and the development of the mother. If you listen to your baby's cries and needs when your infant is young, your child is likely to listen to your instructions later on.

6. *Building a support network*. Use the biblical model of veteran parents teaching novices. The support people around you can be a help in building your intuition or they can be a hindrance.

7. *Boundary building*. Practicing attachment parenting according to God's design implies knowing when to say yes and no to your infant and child. This is why throughout this series of books we emphasize discipline as a major part of Christian parenting.

8. *Balance*. Attachment parenting may sound like one big give-a-thon, in the long run it actually makes parenting a lot easier. The more you give to your child, the more your child gives back to you. Yet, focusing exclusively on your baby's needs and ignoring your own is not wise parenting. Periodically take inventory of your overall style of parenting. Ask yourself "Is it working for me?" and "Am I doing what I need to do for my own well-being?"

Attachment parenting early on makes later parenting easier, not only in infancy but in childhood and in your child's teenage years. The ability to read and respond to your baby carries over to the ability to get inside your child's mind and see things from her perspective. When you truly know your child, parenting is easier at all ages.

I arrived at these principles of attachment parenting not only from parenting eight children with my wife, Martha, but also from observing my patients for twenty years. I also have been encouraged by organizations, such as the La Leche League, that advocate similar parenting principles.

Practicing these principles can help you have a realistic expectation of childhood behavior. You will be more observant of your infant's cues and will be able to respond intuitively. As you become more confident in your ability to meet your baby's needs you will enjoy parenting more and more.

Because of the great variability in family situations, some parents may not be able to practice all of these disciplines all of the time. I just want to make the point that the more parents practice these styles, the greater is their opportunity of truly enjoying their child and of claiming the promise, "Train up a child in the way he should go, / And when he is old he will not depart from it" (Prov. 22:6).

What attachment parenting does for you may be summed up in one word—*harmony*. You and your baby will be more in sync with each other; you will become sensitive to your baby.

Mothers also undergo a chemical change when they have this harmony. Because they are breastfeeding and interacting with their babies, they receive more of the hormone prolactin. I call prolactin "the mothering hormone" because it gives mothers the added boost they need during those trying times.

Attachment parenting also gives your child a model to follow when he or she becomes a parent. Remember, you are parenting someone else's future husband, wife, father, or mother. How your child is parented may influence how he or she parents. The lack of a definite model is what causes confusion in many young parents today.

The principles of attachment parenting are especially rewarding for the parents of "fussy" or "demanding" children whom I like to call "high-need babies." We will be discussing the traits of high-need children and how to parent these special blessings.

There is a parallel between a child's relationship with his parents and his relationship with God. The parental relationship a child has in his early formative years has a direct bearing on his eventual relationship with God. If a child has learned trust, discipline, and love from his parents, he will be prepared to transfer these concepts to God. As you study the tenets of attachment parenting, you will see how to apply them to the spiritual training of your child.

In the following chapters, and in the other books in this series, the disciplines of attachment parenting are covered in great detail. For parents who wish to get the most out of this book, read the entire book through once, and you will see how all these attachment tips fit together. By the end of the book I hope parents will perceive these biblical concepts to be a Christian parenting style that is in accordance with God's design.

Part 1

Your Baby's Emotional Needs

CHAPTER 1

DEVELOPING A PARENTING STYLE THAT WORKS

In the first few weeks of your parenting career you will be bombarded with a barrage of conflicting advice on how to care for your baby. All of your well-meaning friends and relatives are going to offer you their personal how-tos of baby care. Caring for your baby is known as "developing a parenting style." I like to think of a parenting style as a relationship that develops naturally with your baby. From this relationship the how-tos automatically unfold. My dear parents, bear in mind that because you love your baby so much you will be vulnerable to any advice that may claim to make you a better parent or your baby a better child. In this section you will find suggestions on how to evaluate baby-care advice.

My opinion is that God loves us so much that He gives each parent a special intuition to know how to care for and to enjoy his or her child. Implied in this divine design is the law of supply and demand: as long as a parenting style is practiced that allows this intuition to develop, God will supply as much intuition as the child's needs demand. Some parents feel less confident than others, and some children have higher needs than others. I strongly believe that each parent's intuition for child care will match his or her child's needs—but only if the parent allows this relationship to grow according to God's design.

The purpose of this chapter is to help new parents develop a parenting style that is in accordance with God's design. The term *Christian parenting style* means a series of relationships between you and your child that will give you a greater chance of achieving the three primary goals of Christian parenting: (1) knowing your child, (2) helping your child feel right, and (3) leading your child to Christ.

A flurry of books and articles on parenting styles has surfaced in the past twenty years. Titles such as *Choices of Parenting Styles* and *Options for the Busy Parent* convey that new parents can choose a system of child care that fits most conveniently into their own lifestyles. According to these parenting options, parents should identify what lifestyle makes them happiest and then conform their children to it "because children are resilient." I do not feel this style of convenience parenting is in accordance with God's design. Be mindful of the Father's advice: "Train up a child in the way he should go . . ." (Prov. 22:6), meaning the way God has ordained for this child. Seek to determine God's way for your baby. Then help your child grow up in that way even though it may not be the most convenient way.

Another parenting style that is commonly recommended is what I call "restraint parenting." The catch phrases of restraint parenting are: "Don't be so quick to pick up your baby every time he cries"; "Don't let your baby manipulate you"; "What? You're still nursing? You're making him too dependent"; "Don't let your baby sleep with you, she may get into the habit"; "You're going to spoil her"; "You've got to get away from that kid." These common admonitions from trusted advisers to vulnerable new parents only detach parents and babies. Restraint parenting keeps you from knowing your child, keeps your child from feeling right, and ultimately keeps you from fully enjoying your child. Detachment or restraint parenting is not in accordance with God's design.

Attachment Parenting

The style of parenting I sincerely believe is God's design for the father-mother-child relationship is a style I call "attachment parenting." My dear Christian parents, my feelings about conveying this style of parenting to you are so strong that I have spent more hours in prayerful thought on this topic than on any other topic in this book. Attachment parenting is not just my own theory. It is a parenting style I have derived from (1) parenting our own eight children, (2) observing and recording my patients' parenting styles throughout the past twenty years, and (3) becoming involved in parenting organizations whose principles I respect. I have a deep personal conviction that this is the way God wants His children parented. It works!

When discussing attachment, I refer mostly to the mother, not because I feel the father has a minor role in parenting, but because I feel God prefers greater maternal involvement in the first few months of a child's life. However, let me say to fathers that mother-infant attachment is difficult to achieve unless the father is the spiritual leader in a supportive environment. Most of the problems in the parent-child relationship are not a fault in the design or the Designer; they are a result of a total breakdown of the support system that allows a mother to follow God's design.

What is attachment? Mother-infant attachment is a special bond of closeness between mother and baby. This is a unique relationship designed by the Creator to enable the young of the species to reach their fullest potential. I feel that God placed within each mother a type of programming we call "mother's intuition." Some mothers naturally have a more developed intuition; others have to work at developing it, but it is there!

When your child is born, he or she comes complete with a unique set of characteristics we call "temperament." This child also is born with specific needs that, if met, will help modify this temperament and benefit the child's total personality. Some children have higher needs than others. Some children have different sensitive periods for different needs. No two children come wired the same way.

It logically follows that God would not give a certain mother a child whose needs she cannot meet. This is in keeping with what I believe the concept of the Creator to be. God's matching program is perfect; God's law of supply and demand will work, but only if parents develop a parenting style that allows God's design for the parent-child relationship to develop. If parents care for their children according to the divine design, they have a greater chance of claiming the promise, "Train up a child in the way he should go, / And when he is old he will not depart from it" (Prov. 22:6).

Attachment means that mother and baby are in

harmony with each other. Baby gives a cue; mother, because she is open to baby's cues, responds. Baby likes the response and is further motivated to give more cues (because he or she learns he or she will get a predictable response), and the mother-baby pair enjoys each other. They get used to each other. As one attached mother told me, "I'm absolutely addicted to her." Once this happens, the mother's responses become more spontaneous and the how-tos naturally flow. How do you know when you get that attached feeling? When your baby gives you a cue and you respond, if you have a feeling of rightness about your response, and if you are continually sensitive to your baby, you are there. The attachment style of parenting helps you build up your sensitivity.

Why is attachment parenting preferable to restraint parenting? Compare these two styles and the effects they have on parent-child relationships.

Attachment Parenting Advice	*Restraint Parenting Advice*
"Be open to your baby's cues."	"Don't let your baby run your life."
"Take your baby with you."	"You've got to get away from that kid."
"Throw away the clock and the calendar."	"Get that baby on a schedule."
"Respond promptly to cries."	"Let your baby cry it out."
"Travel as a unit."	"You and your husband need to get away."
"Sleep wherever you all sleep best."	"Don't let your baby sleep in your bed; she'll get used to it."

Attachment Parenting Advice

"Let your baby sleep when he is tired."

"Wean when both of you are ready."

"Let her decide when she is ready to be independent."

"Allow discipline to flow naturally from harmony with your baby."

"Let authority flow from trust."

Restraint Parenting Advice

"Put him down at 7:00, and let him cry; he'll learn to sleep."

"What, you're still nursing?"

"You're making her dependent."

"You're spoiling him; he'll never mind."

"She's controlling you."

Attachment Parenting Results

You develop trust and confidence in your parenting intuition.

You know your child better.

You develop realistic expectations.

You adjust more easily to your new lifestyle.

You enjoy your baby more.

You find discipline to be easy.

You find spiritual training to be rewarding.

Restraint Parenting Results

You do not trust your instincts, and you rely on outside advice.

You and your baby have a strained relationship.

You compare your baby to other babies.

You suffer burnout more easily.

You seek alternative fulfillment.

You find discipline to be strained.

You find spiritual training to be stilted.

8

Attachment Parenting Results	*Restraint Parenting Results*
You are more discerning of advice.	You are vulnerable to unwise advice.
You keep pace with your child.	You play catch-up parenting.

Attachment Parenting Results for Your Child	*Restraint Parenting Results for Your Child*
Your child trusts caregivers.	Your child doesn't learn trust.
Your child forms attachments easily.	Your child resists new relationships.
Your child feels right, acts right.	Your child is anxious and dissatisfied.
Your child becomes loving and giving.	Your child becomes withdrawn and restrained.
Your child separates from you easily because he or she was attached to you early.	Your child separates from you with difficulty.
Your child has a good model for his or her own parenting.	Your child is confused about his or her roles as a parent.

An objection to attachment parenting is, "I'm not going to let this tiny baby dominate me; I'll get her on *my* schedule rather than listen to her needs." Being open to your baby's cues does not mean that you are losing control. Being open simply provides the conditions for fully developing your God-given intuition. Openness implies trust in three relationships: (1) you trust your baby to give you the cues to tell you what he needs; (2) you trust yourself and your ability to

9

respond to your baby's cues appropriately; and (3) you trust that God's design for a mother-baby communication network will work if allowed to operate as designed. When your baby cries in the middle of the night (for the third time) and you respond, don't feel you are "giving in"; you are simply giving.

It is important for you to realize that God would not have designed a system of child care that does not work. If you are a mother who says, "I don't feel I have any intuition," respond consistently to your baby without restraint and you will find your shaky intuition maturing. Try to see parenting as a stimulus-response relationship. For example, your baby cries, you pick him up; your baby is restless at night, you sleep with him; your baby enjoys nursing, you don't wean him before his or her time. By freely exercising this stimulus-response relationship, you become more confident in the appropriateness of your response.

What if you are confident in your intuition but are blessed with a very demanding baby (see Chapter 4, "The Fussy Baby")? Again, the law of supply and demand works. Your intuitive response and your perseverance level increase in proportion to your baby's needs. You stay in harmony with each other. However, if you succumb to outside pressure not to be open to your baby, you soon restrain your responses, trust yourself less, and eventually lose harmony with your baby. Restraint parenting leads to a strained parent-child relationship. In subsequent chapters, important attachment principles will be addressed that help the mother-baby relationship develop according to God's design.

Because of the great variability in family situations, you may not be able to practice all of the disciplines of attachment parenting all the time. However, the more these parenting styles are practiced, the greater your chances are of truly enjoying your child.

The Joys of Attachment Parenting

A Harmonious Relationship

What attachment parenting does for you may be summed up in one word: *harmony*. A harmonious relationship allows you and your baby to be more in sync with each other, to become sensitive to each other. You, too, will become addicted to your baby.

A "Hormoneous" Relationship

Attachment parenting also permits you to have a sustained chemical change in your body. Breastfeeding stimulates the hormone prolactin (the milk-producing hormone). This hormone can give you the added boost you need during trying times. I suspect this hormone may be part of the divine design of mother's intuition.

By now, you may be feeling that this attachment style of parenting is all giving, giving, giving. To a certain extent, this is true. Parents are givers and babies are takers; that is how God designed them. Baby's turn to give will come later, and better takers make better givers. But because of this "hormoneous" relationship, baby still can give something back to mother—more prolactin. This mutual giving is a beautiful example of the divine design: mothering stimulates more mothering.

There are nearly two thousand references to "giving" in the Bible. Isn't that what Christianity is all about? Parenting according to God's design helps both parents and children grow to be giving persons.

■ The Baby Bs of Attachment

The eight baby Bs of attachment parenting are:

- ■ birth bonding
- ■ breastfeeding
- ■ babywearing
- ■ bedsharing
- ■ believing in baby's cries
- ■ building a support network
- ■ boundary building
- ■ balance

In the Introduction and in several chapters of *So You're Going to Be a Parent* we discussed the attachment advantages of bonding at birth (chapter 7), breastfeeding your baby (chapter 11), babywearing (chapter 11—babywearing is also discussed more in depth in Chapter 4 of this book). In this book we discuss bedsharing (Chapter 8) and baby's cries (Chapter 2) and throughout our series we talk about the different types of support networks needed from pregnancy through childhood. The two baby Bs that parents often forget and that foster a healthy attachment are boundary building and balance.

Boundary Building

When a baby is between six and nine months old, parents need to be setting limits and making rules. Saying no is as important to bonding as saying yes, but it's vital to understand the child's point of view; I call this approach "getting behind the eyes of the child." By imagining what your child might be feeling when he misbehaves or causes an accident, you can handle the situation in a way that will help your child understand his limits without making him feel he's simply being fussed at. I like to use the take-and-give strategy. For example, you may say to a baby who's doing something you don't want him to, "You may not play with the knife, but you may play with the ball."

You can use this disciplinary tactic as a child grows older. Once, for instance, when our daughter Lauren was two and a half, she spilled juice all over the floor while trying to pour it for herself. Martha knelt beside her and, seeing that Lauren was upset, thought, "If I were Lauren, how would I want my mother to act?" So she simply handed her a rag and the two of them wiped up the mess together. Lauren learned that the proper response to a spill was to just clean it up and also was reminded that her mom was closely attuned to her feelings, thereby strengthening the deep bond they'd already established.

Balance

Parents who focus exclusively on their baby and ignore their own needs get burned out. There may come a time when bonding feels more like bondage.

One woman and her ten-month-old daughter came to our office for counseling. The baby was very clingy, and whined as soon as her mother put her on the floor. At the first peep, her mom scooped the baby up into her arms. The mother's anxiety was reinforcing the child's fussiness.

One of the beauties of being connected is

that your child is able to read your body language. I suggested that this mom try what I call the "no problem, baby" approach. The next time her baby whimpered to be picked up, I advised the mom to turn toward her, briefly acknowledge her with a relaxed, happy face, and resume her adult conversation as if no problem existed. This conveyed an attitude of "You can handle this, Mama's here." After the mother tried this, the child stopped crying and began playing on her own. As the mother learned to balance her own needs with her baby's, she felt more relaxed.

These baby B's are time-tested parenting styles that help you bring out the best in you and your baby. ■

What Can Your Child Expect?

Children who experience attachment parenting exude a feeling of rightness, the basis for a strong self-esteem. If your child feels right about himself, he will be a source of great joy to you. Attachment parenting can give you a better opportunity to enjoy your child.

Attachment parenting also can give your child an appropriate model to follow when he or she becomes a parent. Remember, you are parenting someone else's future husband or wife, father or mother. How your child was parented will influence how he or she parents. The lack of definite models is what causes confusion in many young parents today.

Attachment parenting's real payoff is in caring for what I call the "high-need child." This child goes by many names—the fussy baby, the demanding baby, the strong-willed child—but I prefer the term *high-need child* because it more accurately describes the level of parenting this temperament requires.

God's law of supply and demand works especially well for the high-need child. Attachment parenting increases your parenting energies as your child's needs increase, and you stay in harmony with each other. Restraint parenting may cause you to go out of sync with your baby so that you do not enjoy this special child.

Practicing attachment parenting does not guarantee that your child will not later depart from your teachings. It simply increases the chances that your child will turn out to be a blessing to you. There are three reasons why you cannot claim full credit or blame for your child's future: (1) every child comes wired with a unique temperament; (2) throughout life, your child will be continually bombarded with outside temptations and alternative lifestyles; (3) God has given your child a free will. Comparing child-rearing with planting a seed may help you understand this concept. Certain styles of care give a seed a better chance of bearing good fruit. However, each seed is unique, and the fruit it bears will be vulnerable to the forces of nature. Your child is subject to forces beyond your control, including his or her free will. You can understand why the most well-attached child may bend a bit.

Because God knew children would have erring, human parents, I feel He builds into each child an ability to adjust to a wide range of parenting styles. Most children have a wider acceptance of parenting styles than parents have of their behavior. However, the closer your style of parenting is to God's design, the less your children will tap into their reserves of resilience. As a result, certain undesirable behaviors of childhood that

15

I call "diseases of detachment" are less common (anger, tantrums, depression, withdrawal, distancing).

Attachment parenting lays the foundation for discipline and spiritual training within the first two years of your child's life. Because you know your child better, you are able to assess his or her behavior more accurately and can respond to it more appropriately. Because your child feels right, he or she is more likely to act right. Such an attitude in your child makes punishment seldom necessary, and when necessary, it is administered more appropriately. Because of the attachment you have, both you and your child trust each other. Trust is the basis of authority, and authority makes the final goal of parenting, spiritual training, more effective.

Father Feelings and Mother-Infant Attachment

Occasionally, fathers share these feelings with me: "She's too attached"; "All she does is nurse"; "I feel left out"; "We need to get away alone." These are real feelings from real fathers who sincerely love their children, but feel displaced by them. If you are a father who is feeling displaced, let me assure you that your father feelings and your wife's attachment are very usual and very normal. Perhaps an understanding of God's design for mother-infant attachment and the changes that happen in your wife after birth may help you understand her apparent preference for your baby.

Before she gives birth, a woman's sexual hormones dominate her maternal hormones. After she gives birth, the reverse is true. The maternal hormones increase and stay at high levels for at least six months, during which time a woman's maternal urges may appear to take priority over her sexual urges. This shift of hormones may be part of the divine design to ensure that His young get mothered. A new mother also may feel drained by the incessant demands of her baby, so that by evening she has no sexual inclinations. Mothers commonly describe this feeling as being "all touched out."

A new mother is programmed to be attached to her baby physically, chemically, and emotionally. This does not mean that the father is being displaced by his baby but that some of the energies previously directed toward him are now being directed toward his infant. In time, these energies will be redirected toward the father. Let me share with you an investment tip I have learned in my practice and in my own family: if you are a caring, involved, and supportive husband during this early attachment period, these energies will return to you at a higher level.

I call the early attachment period a "season" of the marriage, a season to parent. If the harvest of this season is tended with care, the season to be sexual will again return.

The Overattachment Syndrome

Be sensitive to the needs of your husband. God designed the family to function as a father-mother-child unit, not as a mother-child unit separate from the father. If you do not have a stable, fulfilled Christian marriage, the father-mother-child relationship ultimately will suffer.

You should not have to choose between your marriage and your child. If both relationships are kept in perspective, both will operate on a higher level. A child should not divide a marriage; a child should be a catalyst to bring husband and wife closer together, if their marriage is God-centered.

The following is a common story about what I call the "overattachment syndrome." Mary and Tom had a reasonably good marriage, but their relationship still needed a lot of maturing and it was not well-founded on Christ. After their baby arrived, Mary tried very hard to be a good mother. Tom was somewhat uncomfortable about handling babies, but he loved his little daughter very much. Mary sensed Tom's uneasy father feelings and was afraid to trust him to comfort the baby when she cried for fear he might upset the baby more. Tom felt more and more left out, and gradually they drifted down separate paths, Mary into her mothering and Tom into his work.

As Mary became more attached to the baby, Tom became more attached to his job and eventually made a few "attachments" of his own. Finally Mary found herself in her pediatrician's office wondering why her marriage was disintegrating. "But I tried to be such a good mother," she said. "My baby needed me. I thought Tom was a big boy and could take care of himself." This common scenario occurs when there is fundamental breakdown in God's order for the family.

Watch out for "red flags" in your attachment relationship: Is the stress causing a division in your marriage? Are you spending less and less time with each other? Is Dad working more and enjoying fathering less? If these red flags are occurring, bring prayer and consultation into your relationship before the diseases of detachment take hold.

Pray daily for your child, for your marriage, and for your parenting relationship. If you bring Christ into your marriage and your parenting relationships, you have a head start toward the attachment mothering and the involved fathering that I sincerely believe are God's order for the Christian family.

■ Spoiling the Spoiling Theory

Babies, like food on a shelf, spoil when they are left alone, not when they are held a lot and responded to. Once upon a time prophets of bad baby advice preached that if you held your baby a lot and responded sensitively to your baby's cries that you would "spoil" your baby or create an overly dependent, manipulative child. Both experience and research have shown the opposite. As long as you respond appropriately to your baby's cues (knowing when to say yes and knowing when to say no) and develop a balance in your attachment style of parenting, you will not spoil your baby.

The spoiling theory is a carryover from the parenting philosophies of nearly a hundred years ago when parents turned over their intuitive childrearing to "experts," who at that time preached restraint parenting along with scientifically produced, artificial baby milk that was supposed to improve upon God's design for feeding babies. There was no scientific basis for the spoiling theory, just unwarranted fears and opinions.

Attachment studies have spoiled the spoiling theory. Two researchers, Drs. Bell and Ainsworth, experts in parent-infant attachment, studied two sets of parents and their children. Group A were attachment-parented babies. Group B babies were

parented in a more restrained way, with a set schedule and given less sensitive responses for their cues. These two groups of babies were tracked for at least a year. Which group do you think eventually turned out to be the most independent? Group A, the securely attached babies. A wise veteran mother who raised lots of godly children once shared her wisdom with us: "Pick them up when they're young, and they'll be more independent when they're older." ■

A Personal Experience

I chose the most attached mother in my practice and asked her to tell what mother-infant attachment has meant to her. The following is what she wrote.

Before birth, a mother and infant are totally attached to each other. Within minutes, birth makes a drastic change in their physical attachment, but in every other way the attachment changes only gradually over a period of years. In some ways, such as emotionally and intellectually, the attachment actually increases. In other ways—functionally and biologically—the attachment takes new forms and gradually lessens.

Immediately after birth the baby and the mother need to remain physically together. Although the physical link between them is severed, the necessity for closeness is intense. The baby needs to be surrounded by familiarity, to be warmed and suckled. The mother needs to be assured that the tiny kicks she had become accustomed to from inside are still there, and that the pregnancy she has "lost" is very surely "found" in the squirming little baby placed on her abdomen. She needs to envelop with her arms and drink in with her eyes and ears the feel, sight, sound, and smell of her newly born child. She needs to marvel at the miracle God has wrought in the depths of her body.

In the first days after birth, the attachment shows itself in new ways. The slightest whimper, the subtlest change in breathing rhythm, or the least shifting of the little body brings the mother to immediate attention. She very quickly responds by drawing her baby close to her, and she feels a rightness flood over her body and mind.

She begins to sleep with "one eye open" in case her baby needs her. If her baby is in a separate room for the night, she sleeps fitfully. She wakes often to listen for his or her cries and often goes in only to find the baby sleeping quietly.

As she performs her daily routine, she keeps her baby near her. If by some chance she discovers her baby has been crying, she is full of remorse that she was not there the instant the baby needed her. The discomfort this brings to her increases her vigilance and her determination that it not happen again. As she settles down to soothe her baby by holding, stroking, crooning, or nursing, a warm feeling of rightness melts away the pain and dismay in a flood of maternal emotions.

The weeks pass, a pattern of attachment develops that is custom-made for the mother and her baby; it is a secret code known and trusted only by the two of them. The father knows and understands this attachment only in part by watching it unfold before him. He develops an attachment of his own to the baby, but it doesn't seem to ease the feeling he has sometimes of being left out of the inner circle around mother and baby. How good it is when he feels secure enough not to interfere with their closeness and not to fee threatened by it.

The father eventually becomes intrigued with the fine-tuning he sees between his wife and their baby. "How did you know?" he'll ask, incredulous that such a subtle clue from the baby (indiscernible to himself) could be so completely and accurately understood by the baby's mother. The mother herself is amazed by her sixth sense about what the baby needs. He doesn't have to cry to let her know he wants to nurse or be picked up or shifted to a change of scene. The baby has a language of gestures, glances, and tiny noises that communicates his needs. The mother and baby are so close, so attached, that the baby seldom cries. The mother has learned to read her baby.

The attachment brings daily discoveries to the mother about herself and about her baby. She finds that if her baby takes an unusually long nap, she begins to yearn for her baby to wake up. She tingles with excitement when she finally notices him or her stirring awake; she has missed her baby and it is good to be reunited.

She makes another discovery in the church nursery, debating with herself whether or not to leave the baby for the first time. She watches other babies being handed over to the nursery workers and put into their assigned slots—one in a swing, one in a crib, one in an infant seat. She pictures herself handing her baby over and considers what instructions she will give. But it doesn't feel right. She watches for a while longer and feels a growing conviction that she should keep her baby with her. As she leaves the nursery with her baby still in her arms, she is relieved the separation hasn't happened.

Another day she discovers that the baby has a finely

developed sense of attachment in terms of measuring acceptable distances. As long as she is within touching distance or within seeing or hearing distance, the baby feels okay. Depending on the baby's need at a particular moment, he or she can tolerate lesser or greater amounts of distance between himself or herself, and his or her mother. Her constant availability enables the baby to develop a trusting nature.

As the baby gets older, the mother feels less urgency in responding to her baby's expressions of need. She feels okay about hurrying through a task, calling "Mom's coming," rather than dropping her work instantly to tend to him or her. Their attachment is now strong enough to handle a slight delay: the mother knows just how long the baby is able to wait before he or she will push the panic button. And these panics rarely occur now that she has learned so much about her baby and about herself as a mother.

A major milestone has been reached, and there will be many others. The attachment that started out to be so total and so intense has changed and will change even more, but there will be one constant thread throughout: the mother and child have a bond that will last a lifetime; it will serve the divine order for both their lives. The mother will have nurtured and the baby will in his or her turn nurture. Their attachment has given birth to human love for generations to come and has guaranteed the fulfillment of God's design for His children.

From Oneness to Separateness

Timely separation is a very important concept. A child must be filled with a sense of oneness with the mother before he or she can develop separateness. A baby must first learn attachment before he or she can handle detachment. A baby must first have a strong identity with his or her mother before he or she can evolve into his or her own self-identity. The age at which babies go from oneness to separateness varies tremendously from baby to baby.

Going from oneness to separateness according to God's design enhances child development. When a baby is securely attached at one stage of development, he more easily progresses to the next stage of development. Eventually the natural desire for independence stimulates the baby to begin to detach gradually from the mother. *It is important that the baby detach from the mother, not the mother from the baby.* For example, a toddler who is just learning to walk cruises farther and farther from his or her mother but periodically turns toward home base to check in. He or she feels secure detaching because his or her mother is there. However, if mother leaves during this separation-sensitive stage, the toddler might become less secure in exploring because home base is gone. Dependence actually fosters independence as long as it happens according to divine design.

Realizing that healthy attachment makes separation easier is good protection against those who insist attachment parenting makes your baby too dependent. Exactly the opposite is true. The baby who is the product of attachment parenting is actually less dependent later. Over the past ten years, research has confirmed what mothers have intuitively known—that early attachment fosters later independence. (I have summarized these scientific studies in my book *Growing Together*, published by La Leche League International, Schaumberg,

Illinois, 1987.) The concept of oneness to separateness has long been appreciated in secular books on child care. Unfortunately, it has not been understood among writers of Christian child-care books.

When Can I Leave My Baby?

If your attachment parenting has been practiced according to divine design, you will not want to leave your baby. You will probably experience some withdrawal symptoms the first time you leave your baby. For example, I see new mothers peering through the window the first time they leave their babies in the church nursery. They are not being possessive, which means keeping a child from doing what he needs to do because of some personal need. They are simply being attached. If you are a new mother and you feel a continual urge to get away from your baby, I advise you to pray and seek counsel because very often this desire implies some departure from God's design. You should enjoy being with your baby so much that, although an occasional outing may seem necessary, you really have difficulty being away from him or her.

How often and at what age a mother leaves her baby depends on many variables, including her need to get away. You may honestly feel you need occasional relief. If you feel a need to be refilled by some outside interest, follow your desire; an empty mother is no good to anyone, especially her baby. Oftentimes your restlessness will not be the need to get away from your baby, but the need for a change of scenery. Consider taking your baby along. You may feel you're not the stay-at-home type. "Home" to a tiny baby is where his mother is; take your baby out. God's design is for mother and baby to be tied together, not tied down.

The divine design is a bond, not a bondage. When planning a time to be apart from your baby, the following questions need to be considered.

How separation-sensitive is your baby? Some babies separate more easily than others because of their individual temperaments.

What is your baby's need level? High-need babies separate with difficulty; they are designed that way.

Who is the substitute caregiver? When you leave your baby, be sure to give explicit instructions on how you want your baby mothered in your absence. For example, tell the caregiver, "When she cries, I want you to pick her up immediately and comfort her." If possible, try to leave your baby during his or her prime time, which is the mornings for most babies. Try not to leave your baby during fussy times when he or she needs your nurturing.

As you grow in your attachment style of parenting you will develop a finely tuned sense of your baby's needs and how to respond to them. A baby's cry is the method she uses to communicate her needs and is distinct according to her specific need. Learning to discern and properly respond to your baby's cries is the task that will consume your first weeks as a parent.

CHAPTER 2

HOW TO RESPOND TO YOUR BABY'S CRIES

■ "Should I let my baby cry?" is one of the most common questions new parents ask. More wrong advice is given by the Christian community about this question than about any other aspect of parenting. To illustrate the confusion, let me share the responses to a questionnaire I recently sent to a group of Christian parents.

The questionnaire pertained to parenting styles. One of the questions was, "What advice do friends and relatives give you about what to do when your baby wakes up crying in the middle of the night?" Most of the parents answered that they received restraint parenting advice: "Let him cry it out"; "She must learn to be independent"; "Don't pick her up, or you might spoil her"; "You are creating a habit if you come every time he cries."

In response to the question, "How do you feel about the 'let your baby cry' type of advice?" I received the following answers: "I can't let her cry when I know that I have the means to comfort her"; "It goes against my instinct"; "It just doesn't feel right to me"; "It would drive me nuts if I let him cry"; "I feel so guilty if I let her cry."

The difference between what parents hear and what they intuitively feel illustrates that there is a lot of confusion about how to respond to a crying baby. In this chapter, I will present what I feel is God's design for this special type of communication.

A Baby's Cry Is a Baby's Language

A mother once said to me, "If only my baby could talk, I would know what she wants." I responded, "Your baby can talk, you just have to learn how to listen." Throughout the Old Testament are more than one hundred references to how people communicate with God through crying. Psalm 72:12, for example, says, "He will deliver the needy when he cries." In these biblical passages crying conveys need and a trust that crying will be heard.

The crying communication between a mother and her baby is very similar to the cries throughout Scripture. A baby has genuine needs. When he calls out to someone whom he trusts, he confidently expects an appropriate response. This section will show you how to develop this communication network so that an appropriate response to your baby's cry benefits both you and your baby.

Develop a Sensitivity to Your Baby's Cries

In their first few months, babies cry a lot because they need a lot. Their needs are high, but their ability to communicate them is low. When they are three to four months old, babies are attempting to adjust to their new environments. During this adjustment period, they are very sensitive; some are more sensitive than others. Babies who have difficulty adjusting to their new environments are called "fussy babies," "colicky babies," or, as I like to call them, "high-need babies." Sensitivity characterizes these babies. They signal their normal biological needs and their sensitivities by crying. The key to modifying their behavior is for their parents and other caregivers to develop their own sensitivities.

Every new mother has a built-in receiver to her baby's cries. The more she allows herself to respond spontaneously and promptly to her baby's cries, the more sensitive she becomes to her baby. And the more sensitive she becomes, the more intuitively she responds. When a mother says to me, "I can't stand to let her cry," she is showing that she has built up her sensitivity.

Becoming a sensitive parent is an indication that you are becoming a sensitive Christian. Part of your development as a Christian is to become sensitive to others' needs. If someone is in need and is hurting, your inner sensitivity drives you to respond to that person's needs. The compassion of Jesus is a recurring theme in Scripture.

The physiological changes that occur in a new mother's body when she hears her baby cry further illustrate that it is God's design for her to respond promptly to her baby's cries. In response to her own baby's cries, the blood flow to a mother's breasts increases, often accompanied by the urge to nurse. This is a biological clue that God designed a mother to pick up her baby (and usually nurse him) when he cries.

How a mother and baby develop their crying communication network is a forerunner to building another important aspect of their relationship: trust. Their trust is interrelated: the baby trusts his mother to respond to his cries; the mother trusts her baby to communicate his needs; and she learns to trust her ability to meet his needs.

How to Trust Your Response to Your Baby's Cries

The more you exercise a skill, the more skillful you become; the more promptly and appropriately you respond to your baby's cries, the more confident you become in your ability to comfort your baby. When a mother picks up and nurses her crying baby, she will observe the peaceful feeling her prompt response gives her baby. This immediate gratification of her consoling efforts creates a feeling of rightness within her. This further increases her confidence and trust in herself.

To reassure parents of high-need babies it must be stated that some babies are not as easily consoled as others, not because of their parents' abilities but be-. cause of their own sensitive temperaments. If a baby does not stop crying when she is picked up and consoled, a new parent's confidence is absolutely shaken. Some very sensitive babies cry a couple of hours each day of their first few months, no matter how experienced their caregivers are. If you have been blessed with a baby whose cries are not easily consoled, God will give you the strength and ability to console your sensitive baby, providing you do not interfere with His design. The conditions of this design are that you continually remain open to your baby and promptly respond to his cries. Eventually you will be able to supply the comforting measures necessary to meet your baby's demands.

Parents who persevere through prayer eventually can comfort their babies. One mother of a high-need baby shared with me, "When he becomes unglued, I now feel I can help him pull himself back together. It has been a long, tough struggle, but I feel I am finally beginning to cash in on all my efforts." This mother is saying that she trusts herself because she has let herself be open to the conditions that allowed her trust to develop.

What Can Your Baby Expect?

Because the mother and father are learning to trust their parenting abilities, the baby is learning trust also. Trust is a prime determinant for developing harmony in the parent-child relationship. The more you trust your infant's signals, the more he learns to trust them. By your believing that your baby cries because he has a need, not because he is manipulating you, your infant trusts that you trust his cues. The more you respond to his cues, the more he trusts his developing ability to signal his needs. This trust is the forerunner of his developing self-esteem.

Put yourself in your baby's place. When his cries are answered, he probably feels, "I trust that my cries will be consistently, predictably, and appropriately responded to; therefore, I am a special person. When I cry, someone listens. Therefore, my message must be getting through."

31

■ Beware of Baby Trainers

Once you have a new baby, you become a target for baby trainers all touting their magic formulas for raising babies. Remember, this is your baby and you are her parents. Be discerning about using someone else's techniques to care for your baby. "Training up your child in a way he should go" implies knowing which way he should go, which means discovering your baby's unique temperament, qualities, and developing a parenting style that brings out these qualities. Avoid what we call "the sheep syndrome," blindly following false teachings or prophets with bad baby advice.

Trust your intuition. God would not have given you a child without also giving you the built-in wisdom to care for this child. Keep experimenting with your individual style of parenting until you find the one that works for you. ■

How to Respond to Your Baby's Cries

From the day she is born, regard your baby's crying as communication, not as a habit to be broken. This starts your parent-baby communication network off on the right "ear." Be open to your baby; take a risk. With time, your ability to interpret your baby's cries will get easier and easier because you have allowed yourself the openness to let this communication network develop the way God designed it to work.

You may take a little longer to interpret your baby's cries, and your baby may take a little longer to respond to your comforting measures, but you two will get together as long as you do not do anything to interfere with God's design for the natural development of this special communication network. When your baby cries, respond spontaneously, intuitively, and freely to the first little blip that comes in on your radar system.

If you feel the urge to analyze your response to your baby's cry in a given situation, analyze your response after and not before you respond. If you wait until you have figured it out, you take this beautiful communication network out of the realm of an intuitive art and put it into a science, and the science of "cryology" simply does not exist. A baby's cry is her own unique language. No two people talk the same, no two babies cry the same. No two mother-baby units are wired the same.

The After-Cry Feeling

After you have responded intuitively to your baby's cries, examine your feelings. If you feel right, then you made the right decision and responded appropriately. If you have not responded appropriately, you will not feel right. The feeling of rightness or nonrightness after you respond to your baby's cries is part of a crying-consciousness that goes into your maturity as a parent.

To understand this concept, consider your crying-consciousness to be similar to an inner computer in which a certain stimulus, your baby's cry, is matched with a certain response, your quickness and appropriateness of response to his cry. Picture yourself with several response buttons that are labeled (1) red alert, respond immediately; (2) hold off a bit; and (3) sit tight, grin and bear it. When you press the response button that matches your baby's crying signal, your feeling of rightness is like an "okay" light that comes on in your computer. If the stimulus-response network is not in harmony with your baby, a feeling of un-rightness is the result and a sort of "guilt" light comes on. This accounts for feeling guilty when you let your baby cry. It is a healthy guilt that means you have developed an inner sensitivity, a crying-consciousness that has told you your response was not appropriate and needs to be refined.

I feel that God puts this crying-consciousness into a mother for the survival of the baby and the development of the mother. It is the unwillingness to listen to this crying-consciousness that gets new parents in trouble.

How you respond to your baby's cries in the middle of the night is an example of this crying-consciousness. Suppose your baby awakens from a very deep sleep. This usually means that the stimulus that is waking him is very strong. As a result, he cries a piercing "I need immediate attention" kind of cry. Your "red alert" or jump-up-and-respond light goes on; you settle your baby, and everybody feels right about it.

Another type of middle-of-the-night cry is the set-tling cry a baby makes when he is in transition from one state of sleep to another or when he is adjusting his sleeping position. This cry is usually of low intensity and is neither unsettling to your baby nor alarming to you. The cry lasts a few minutes and quickly diminishes. This type of crying stimulus usually matches well with your "hold off" button, and your baby often settles himself back to sleep without any outside help. Because your stimulus-response network was in harmony, your "okay" light goes on and a feeling of rightness results.

If, however, your baby emits a persistent, high-intensity cry and you press the "grin and bear it" button, you will be left with a feeling of unrightness and your "guilt" light will go on. If this happens, listen and learn from the feeling of unrightness that results, and the next time a similar cry appears, push the right button.

If you continue to push the wrong button, insensitivity results. When it comes to responding appropriately to your baby's cries, no third-party adviser can push the right button for you. Your baby's crying circuitry is wired into your computer, nobody else's.

Repeating this stimulus–response–right-feeling cycle further develops your inner sensitivity and crying-consciousness as you both mature in your relationship.

The Ultimate in Harmony

One intuitive mother who had developed a very sensitive crying-consciousness said to me, "Isn't it a shame that a baby always has to cry to get whet he needs." The ultimate design for harmony between you and your baby is for you to be so tuned in to your baby's cues that he does not necessarily have to cry to get attention. The more you follow the attachment style of parenting, the more often you will reach this sensitivity.

Parents who always have their radar systems tuned in toward their babies often can sense when they are hungry just by the looks on their faces or by how they act. Attachment parents are also always on the lookout for stress indicators and often will respond before their older babies start crying. For example, when our baby, Erin, looks up at me with raised arms, she is signaling, "Daddy, pick me up." If I pick her up, no cry results. If I miss her opening cue, next follows a cry. I have never had a particularly high tolerance for a baby's cries. In our home, we have found it much more pleasant to create an atmosphere in which our babies usually do not have to cry to get what they need.

A behaviorist may object that if you pick up a baby every time she lifts her arms to you, you are spoiling the baby. Let me offer an alternative viewpoint. If you respond to your baby's signals before your baby has to cry, you are reinforcing those signals instead; whereas, if you let your baby cry, you are teaching him or her that babies who are left to cry learn to cry harder; babies who are responded to promptly learn to cry better.

Restraint parenting is common, especially in Christian circles. I want to address this issue point by point in the next chapter for the benefit of those who advise new parents to allow their children to cry.

CHAPTER 3

AN UNWISE PARENTING STYLE: RESTRAINT PARENTING

■ Leaving babies to cry is a carryover from the fifties and sixties. Parents in this generation worried that their children would run their lives or manipulate them. Schedules, formulas, and checklists were in vogue. Parents wanted quick and easy answers to difficult child-rearing problems.

This mode of parenting accounts for one of the most popular and, unfortunately, still prevalent pieces of advice concerning the child who wakes up during the night: "Let your baby cry for three nights and on the fourth night he will sleep." Not only does this advice usually not work, but quick-result parenting is an unrealistic expectation.

"You Might Spoil Him"

Spoiling is one of those words that has crept into baby books over the years but never should have. Spoiling implies something has not been attended to properly; it was left alone, put on a shelf and left to rot.

Actually, restraint parenting is more apt to spoil children than attachment parenting.

Spoiling originated with restraint parenting, which teaches that if you respond to your child's cries when he is an infant, you will create a whiny child who cries when he doesn't get his way. Several studies have confirmed that infants whose cries are promptly responded to actually cry less when they are older.

"You Must Discipline Your Baby"

Discipline is another goal of the "let your baby cry" advice. This idea is also a carryover from the sixties when discipline was confused with control. If you responded promptly to your baby, your baby was controlling you, and you were losing your authority.

Many Christian parents were drawn to this concept of control. Books on how to discipline children flooded the Christian book market, and if someone wanted to be guaranteed a large audience to a talk on parenting, the speaker would always put *discipline* in the title. Parents cried (especially those who practiced restraint parenting), "I don't know how to discipline my child." What they really were saying was, "I don't *know* my child." They had restrained themselves from listening to their babies' cries, had failed to communicate with them, and were unable to establish discipline.

"It's Good for a Baby's Lungs"

Another bit of erroneous advice is that crying is good for a baby's lungs. To my knowledge, crying has no beneficial effect on a baby's lungs. In fact, some babies often turn blue when crying hard, and older children may hold their breath and faint while crying uncontrollably.

Negative Effects of Restraint Advice

Restraint advice goes against a mother's instinct. A mother is not designed to let her baby cry, and a baby is not designed to be left to cry. When God's design for this crying-consciousness is not followed, disharmony results in the mother-baby relationship. Mothers, have faith in your God-given instinct. If any advice runs counter to your inner feeling of rightness about a certain piece of advice, don't follow it.

There may be in every person an instinct to respond to a crying baby. Even two year olds instinctively respond to the cries of their newborn siblings. For example, a mother brought her twenty-two-month-old daughter and her one-month-old baby for a well-baby exam. As soon as the newborn baby began to cry, the older child pleaded, "Quick, Mommy, pick baby up." The mother then said to me, "She always feels this way. I can't get to her baby sister fast enough."

Restraint Advice Is Presumptuous

When a mother has been advised to let her baby cry, other people are presuming that they know why her baby is crying. But they don't. They are presuming that the baby is crying to manipulate or to annoy and that he really does not need to cry. This is unfair and untrue. Others are presuming that nothing is really wrong with the baby, but they do not have the facts to warrant such a conclusion. They are also presuming that the mother would be better off if she let the baby cry, which is also untrue. Finally, they are presuming to know better than the mother knows why the baby is crying. This is not true, since they probably have no biological attachment to that baby and are not near him at 3:00 A.M. when he cries. Outsiders have neither a harmonious nor a "hormoneous" relationship with that baby. In essence, they do not qualify as baby advisers. This kind of advice is unfair to the baby, unconstructive to the mother, and basically unchristian. "Be kind to one another" (Eph. 4:32).

I do not wish to offend the new parents' friends or relatives who may be reading this section. I am sure you mean well and sincerely care about the well-being of both mother and baby, but I wish you to consider the effects of your advice before offering it. Keep in mind that the new parents, especially the mother, are vulnerable to any child-care advice because they love their child so deeply. Their love is coupled with natural concern that they do not do anything harmful to their baby. Even though allowing their baby to cry goes against their inner wisdom, they may feel unsettled and think, *We will not be good parents if we don't follow this advice* or *Our child may be affected harmfully if we don't let our baby cry.*

The "Let your baby cry" advice is probably the most counterproductive advice in child rearing. It creates within the mother a dilemma and a confusion between what she hears and what she feels. The writers and preachers who continue to teach restraint parenting should reassess whether or not their doctrine is in accordance with God's design.

Restraint Advice Desensitizes the New Parent

I sympathize with parents who fall prey to restraint advice. One day I was sitting in our backyard reading a psychology book on reinforcement of behavior (which indeed is a valid concept as long as one uses discernment in deciding what is reinforcement of negative behavior and what is restraining a response to normal behavior). While I was reading this book, I was generally in a restraining mood toward any child's behavior because this was the topic of the book. Our little one year old, Erin, cruised by on her bike and tumbled off into the soft grass. She certainly did not appear to be hurt, but she started whimpering a bit. Her whimper steadily increased to an all-out cry. During the development of this crying syndrome, I was heavily involved in the mental gymnastics of *Is she crying because of habit or need? Will I be reinforcing negative behavior? Will she be manipulating me?* As I was thinking these ridiculous thoughts, Erin looked over at me as only an infant can do, with a look on her face that said, "Dad, cut the psychology. Follow your instincts and come over here and pick me up." I eventually did, and we both felt right. Perhaps Erin was telling me to quit doing so much reading and start doing more intuitive fathering.

Restraint Parenting Encourages Mistrust

If you trust that your child is crying because she has a need, your child learns to trust her ability to give cues and to trust that her cues will be appropriately and consistently responded to. When you use a nonresponding (or nonresponsible) approach, you are using the principles of nonreinforcement: if you do not reinforce the behavior, the behavior soon stops. This is a popular psychological principle that is valid if it is controlled.

Sometimes this principle of reinforcement becomes too behavioristic and bothers me for two reasons: (1) it assumes the baby's crying is negative behavior, which is a false assumption, and (2) this approach may have a damaging effect on the baby's emerging self-esteem. If a baby's action elicits a positive reaction, he is further motivated to develop better communication skills with his responder, meaning that he is motivated to communicate with his caregiver in a noncrying way.

Occasionally a parent will report, "But it works . . . he stopped crying." I have questioned several hundred parents about how they respond to crying, and for the majority, the restraint approach does not work. Let's analyze the possible effects of this restraint on the babies for whom this approach works.

By not responding to your baby when he cries in the night, you are not really teaching your baby to sleep; you are teaching him that his inner form of communication is ineffective. He may fall back to sleep, but he has to withdraw from the disappointment of not being listened to. By not giving in to your baby, you are teaching your baby to give up. I have my doubts about the wisdom of this approach.

Parents who have restrained themselves from responding to their babies' cries often report that when they later pick up their babies, they feel the infants withdraw from them. They sense a feeling of "baby anger." What the babies are exhibiting and the parents are feeling is basically a sense of disharmony, that God's design for parent-infant response was ignored.

Responding as a Role Model

Responding to your crying baby models a parenting style for your older children. How they see you parent a new baby has a great effect on their own future parenting styles. The importance of modeling became evident to us one day when Martha and I were in the kitchen and we heard our daughter Erin crying from our bedroom. As we started toward the bedroom, we heard her crying stop. When we reached the bedroom, we saw a beautiful sight: our sixteen-year-old son, Jim, a big, athletic boy, was lying down next to Erin, gentling and consoling her. Why was Jim doing this? Because he had learned from us that when a baby cries, someone listens.

CHAPTER 4

THE FUSSY BABY: ALIAS THE HIGH-NEED CHILD

God has "blessed" some parents with a particularly difficult baby who is known by various titles, such as "fussy," "demanding," or "exhausting." As these babies grow older they acquire additional labels, such as "hyperactive" or "strong-willed." I prefer to call this kind of baby "the high-need child." This is not only a kinder term, but it more accurately describes what these children are like and the level of parenting they need. Since understanding increases acceptance, it is important to understand why high-need babies fuss and why you react the way you do. Also included in this section are some survival tips for exhausted parents.

Do not be too quick to judge from your baby's temperament the person he or she later will become. Many difficult babies turn out to be even-tempered children. There is a wide range of temperaments among babies. This section is to be read as a general guide; some of this advice may apply to you and some may not.

■ Babywearing: Why It's Good to Carry Your Baby a Lot

Babies fuss and parents comfort. That's a realistic fact of new family life. Developing your skills as a baby-comforter will be a top priority as a new parent. Comforting a fussy baby can be as easy as taking an afternoon walk around the room or as hard as seemingly climbing a mountain at 2:00 A.M. Beginning in the early weeks, wear your infant in a sling for as many hours a day as you and your baby enjoy. Once you and your baby master this age-old custom of baby-mellowing, a babysling will be one of your most useful parenting tools, and you won't want to leave home without it. Here is why.

Sling Babies Cry Less

Infant-development researchers who study baby-care practices in America and other cultures have reported that the more infants are carried, the less they fuss. In fact, research has shown that babies who are carried at least three hours a day cry 40 percent less than infants who aren't carried as much. Over the years in pediatric practice, we have listened to and watched veteran baby-calmers and have heard a recurrent message: "As long as I have my baby in my arms or on my body, she's content." This observation led us to popularize the term *babywearing*.

"Wearing" means more than just picking up baby and putting him in a carrier when he fusses. It means carrying baby many hours a day *before* baby needs to fuss. Mothers who do this tell us: "My baby seems to forget to fuss."

Being nestled in a sling is like an outside womb. The mother's walking motion reminds baby of the rhythm he enjoyed in the womb. The sling encircles and contains the infant who would otherwise become agitated and waste energy flinging arms and legs around. The carried baby is only a breath away from his mother's or father's voice, familiar sounds he has grown to associate with feeling good. Babies settle better in this live environment than they do when parked in swings or plastic infant seats.

The physiological reason why carried babies are more content and less colicky is because this style of parenting promotes *quiet alertness*—the behavior state in which babies behave best. Besides calming babies, wearing enhances learning. A carried baby is intimately involved in the world of the parents. When a mother is on the phone, baby hears what she says. When a father wears baby through the supermarket, being up in arms gives baby a visual advantage.

Babywearing Enhances Parent-Infant Bonding

Familiarity breeds content. Being nestled in a familiar position is especially calming for the baby who is easily distracted and falls apart at the first sign of a strange person or strange place. From this secure position, the baby has less fear of the unfamiliar.

Babywearing is especially useful for day-care providers. Susan, a mother in our practice, had a high-need baby, Erin, who was content as long as she was in a sling; but Susan had to return to work when Erin was six weeks of age. I wrote the following prescription to give to her daycare provider: "To keep baby content, wear her in a sling at least three hours a day." For high-need babies, the "womb" lasts eighteen months: nine months inside, and nine months outside.

Babywearing is especially useful for parents who are on the go a lot. Some mothers have the type of job that allows them to take their babies with them, at least in the early months—a style we call "work and wear." Our receptionist wore her baby to work for the first six months. A baby learns a lot in the arms of a busy parent.

As we were studying parenting styles that work best for most parents most of the time, we interviewed mothers from other cultures who traditionally wear their babies in slings for several hours a day. These cultures are renowned for their intuitive mothering and calm babies. We asked them why women in their cultures wear their babies most of the time. The usual responses were: "It makes life easier for the mother" and "It's good for the baby." Those are the two simple things that parents around the world really want. We predict that during the next decade you will see fewer strollers and more slings. It's a great time to be a baby. ■

Profile of a High-Need Baby

I have pulled from my gallery of high-need babies the following personality traits that mothers have shared with me about their babies.

"He is supersensitive." High-need babies are keenly aware of changes in their environments. Most babies are endowed with stimulus barriers that allow them to filter out disturbing stimuli and receive pleasant experiences selectively. This process is called "adaptability." Sensitive babies have more permeable stimulus barriers. They startle easily during the day and settle with difficulty at night. These babies appeal to their parents to provide the security and stimulus barriers they cannot provide for themselves.

"I just can't put him down; he wants to be held all the time." These babies crave physical contact and are not known for their self-soothing abilities. New parents often have unrealistic expectations that their babies will lie quietly in their cribs, and play attentively with dangling mobiles, gazing passively at interested onlookers. This is certainly not the play profile of the high-need baby. These babies are most content in their parents' arms and at their mothers' breasts.

"He is so intense." Fussy babies spend a lot of energy on their behavior. They feel things more intensely and express their feelings more forcefully. They cry with gusto and are quick to protest if their needs are not met.

"He wants to nurse all the time." The term *feeding schedule* is not in these babies' vocabulary. They need prolonged periods of nonnutritive sucking and do not wean easily.

"He is hypertonic and uncuddly." While most babies mold easily into the arms of caregivers, some high-need babies arch their backs and stiffen their arms and legs in protest at any attempt to cuddle them.

"He awakens frequently." A tired mother lamented, "Why do high-need babies need more of everything but sleep?" These babies carry their general

sensitivity into their naptime and nighttime. They seem to be constantly alert as if they have been endowed with internal lights that are always turned on and not easily turned off. Parents often describe their special babies as "tiring but bright." This brightness is usually what keeps high-need babies awake.

"He is unpredictable." Unpredictability is another behavior trait of these special babies. High-need babies are inconsistently appeased. What works one day often does not work the next. One exhausted father exclaimed, "Just as I think I have the game won, she just keeps upping the ante."

"He is demanding." High-need babies are certainly demanding. They convey a sense of urgency to their signals. "Red alerts" dominate their crying vocabulary. They have no respect for delayed gratification and do not readily accept alternatives. They are quick to protest if their needs are not met or if their cues have been misread. Their incessant demands account for a common complaint from their parents: "I feel drained."

This profile of the high-need baby may appear to be predominantly negative, but it is only part of the natural history of parenting these special babies. I advise professional counseling for all parents of high-need babies. Those who have had professional counseling and who practice the attachment style of parenting gradually begin to see their babies in a different light and use more positive descriptions such as "challenging," "interesting," and "bright." Parents of high-need babies need to realize that the same exhausting qualities that first seem to be liabilities are likely to become assets for their children. The intense baby may become the creative child; the sensitive infant, the compassionate child; and the little taker may become the big "giver."

The Need-Level Concept

A high-need baby can bring out the best and the worst in a parent. I believe that part of the divine design for the parent-child relationship is what I call the "need-level concept," a concept designed to bring out the best in both parent and child.

Every child comes wired with a certain temperament that is determined primarily by genetics and is influenced somewhat by the womb environment. The child also needs a certain level of care proportional to his temperament in order that he fit well into his environment. Some babies need a higher level of care than others. In order to signal the level of care he needs, a baby has the ability to give cues to signal his needs. Part of the divine design is that babies with higher needs give stronger cues. High-need babies come wired with the ability to extract from their caregiving environments the necessary comforting measures to satisfy their needs. For example, a baby who needs to be carried all the time will cry if he is not carried enough. This is how he merits the label "demanding."

Parents should view the term *demanding* as a positive character trait that has developmental benefits for their baby. If a baby were endowed with high needs yet lacked the corresponding ability to signal her needs, her developmental potential would be threatened and her emerging self-esteem would be in jeopardy. I feel high-need babies are naturally demanding in order to extract a level of care needed to reach their maximum potential.

How does a parent measure up to the incessant demands from the high-need baby? Another part of the need-level concept is that the needs a baby signals bring out the nurturing responses of his parents. As babies come wired with certain temperaments, mothers also are endowed with certain nurturing responses. For some mothers, nurturing develops proportionately to their babies' needs. For others, nurturing is not so automatic and needs maturing. I do not believe God would give parents a baby with greater needs than they can meet. This would not fit with the concept of Creator; God's matching program is perfect. Keep in mind God's law of supply and demand: God will supply you with the level of energy you need to meet your baby's demands providing you seek His help in practicing the style of parenting that allows this to happen.

■ Baby Comfort, Dad-Style

One night during our early years of parenthood, the baby started fussing. Martha was out for the evening, so I had to handle things myself. I tried all the standard strategies to calm our child down, but nothing worked—until I nestled the baby's head under my chin and began walking slowly around the room humming "Old Man River." The baby soon dozed off, and I realized I had just experienced a memorable father-baby moment.

That was the night I invented the *neck nestle*. This technique did more than just quiet our little one; it gave me a boost of confidence in my fathering abilities.

The challenge of comforting an upset baby has long been relegated to the mother. And, since mothers take to soothing crying infants so naturally, fathers often shy away from sharing in the comforting rituals. This creates a lose-lose-lose situation. Mom misses the support of her mate and the relief he can offer her from primary caregiving responsibilities—making her prone to burnout. Baby misses the opportunity to get to know and enjoy Dad's unique way of comforting. And Dad forfeits the chance to learn, by trial and error, what comforting techniques work best.

When it comes to comforting a fussy baby, mothers may have certain biological advantages over fathers. A mother's body is built to nurture and respond to her baby in special ways—by breastfeeding, for example. But the fact is that dads are also biologically equipped to comfort a crying baby in unique ways.

Whether by choice or necessity, more and more fathers today are taking an active role in caring for their babies. And by developing their natural parenting gifts, fathers create a special bond with their infants—and their wives. Here are some father-tested comforting techniques that I have used to soothe our fussy babies (and make points with Martha).

Neck Nestle

While walking, dancing, or lying with your baby on your chest, snuggle her head against the front of your neck and drape your chin over the baby's head. Then hum or sing a low-pitched melody, such as "Old Man River," while swaying from side to side. With the neck nestle, Dad has an edge over Mom because of the lower-pitched sound of the male voice. Babies hear through the vibrations of their skull bones as well as their ears, and in the neck nestle your baby's skull rests against your voice box. If you hum or sing while holding your infant this way, the slower, more easily felt vibrations of your voice will often lull baby right to sleep. As an added attraction, your baby's scalp will be pleasantly warmed by the air you exhale.

Warm Fuzzy

The warm fuzzy is another high-touch soother where a father can really shine. Dads, lie down and drape your baby skin-to-skin over your chest, placing baby's ear over your heart. The rhythm of your heartbeat and the up-and-down motion of your breathing will relax your baby. As she drowses, those tiny fists will uncurl and her limbs will dangle limply over your chest.

Football Hold

Tucking a colicky infant under your arm like a football is particularly effective for soothing abdominal discomfort when your baby is tense and gassy. Drape your baby's stomach down over your forearm, with her head in the crook of your elbow, and her legs straddling your hand. Then, grasp the diaper area firmly while your forearm presses on baby's tense abdomen.

Fathering Down

To survive and thrive with a high-need baby, both parents must share daytime and nighttime parenting. But even the most experienced mothers tend to fall into solo nighttime parenting and don't ask their husbands for help.

Here are some ways to "father" your baby to sleep, even during the fussiest moments. If your infant isn't quite ready for dreamland (though you might be!), put her in a babysling and wear her as you stroll around the house until she falls into a deep sleep, which takes about twenty minutes from when she first nods off. Then make your way to baby's bed, bend over, and ease yourself out of the sling while lowering the baby onto the mattress. If baby stirs and resists being patted off to sleep, go back to the sling a little while longer. Or, lie down yourself with baby still in the sling, as in the warm fuzzy. With the rhythm of your breathing and heartbeat, sleep will soon overtake your little one.

A Note to Moms

While your mate works on developing his baby-comforting skills, your job is to set him up to succeed. The usual maternal instinct is to rush over and rescue a fussy baby from her fumbling daddy. This not only gives your mate the message that he's incompetent at baby care, but it also deprives Dad of the opportunity to refine his comforting techniques.

So, let Dad take over. Be sure your infant is well fed, and confidently hand him off to your husband. Then take a walk, go shopping—take some time to yourself—and give Daddy and baby some space to develop their relationship and work out their own comforting system. ■

Survival Tips for Parenting the Fussy Baby

The following survival tips are designed to help you comfort your baby and yourselves.

Don't Feel Guilty

Many new mothers think, *What am I doing wrong?* or *I'm not a good mother,* when their babies are fussy. However, the "goodness" of their babies is not a measure of their effectiveness as mothers. Babies fuss because of their own temperaments, not because of their mothers' abilities.

Your fussy baby can shake your confidence as a new mother and absolutely destroy many of the rewarding aspects of parenting. The less confident you become, the less you are able to comfort your baby's needs and the more inconsolable he becomes. This cycle often results in escape mothering, an unfortunate break in the continuum of parenting. This tendency to want to escape when the going gets tough is often a normal reaction to relieve your guilt and preserve your sanity.

Remember, your responsibility is not to make your baby stop crying—your responsibility is to comfort him to the best of your ability, seeking any means that may help until things get better. Your baby may still cry but you are responding and you are not leaving him to cry alone. Your baby needs you to be strong and to be there for him. He doesn't need you to hush him just because his crying is aggravating or upsetting you.

Try to pinpoint whether his crying makes you feel desperate or helpless or panicked, and try to discover why you may be feeling this way. Your anguish of heart may be rooted in very early pain you experienced when you were left to cry it out as a baby. Take a deep breath, pray, and ask the Lord to heal that. Then, carry on comforting.

My heart goes out to mothers who hang tough in

the compassionate care of their fussy babies. Their reward will be great both on earth and in heaven.

Learn to Accept Your Blessing

Parents of fussy babies need to develop a high level of acceptance. In counseling parents of fussy babies I often start with, "You have been blessed with . . ." Quite frankly, by the time many parents come in for counseling they feel anything but blessed and would be happy if God would take their little "blessing" back.

I tell them, "You have been blessed with a baby of high-need levels. God has blessed you with a special child, and He will help you become special parents." In many instances, our Creator has matched the temperaments of mothers and babies so that a fussy baby may have a mother with a high level of acceptance. Occasionally a family may have a fussy baby and a mother with a low level of acceptance. This high-risk situation needs much prayer and consultation.

The law of supply and demand. I have faith in the divine design that God would not bless you with a baby who demands more than you are able to give. Your level of giving will increase if you fulfill the conditions that allow God's design to work, such as the attachment style of parenting covered earlier.

Fussiness is often in the eyes of the beholder. I often refer new parents who feel they have a fussy baby to parents who have coped successfully with a fussy child. After meeting with these parents, the new parents often exclaim, "Praise the Lord, we don't have a fussy baby after all." Parental expectations of what babies are like are often not realistic. When parents understand more about the differences in temperament among babies, they can accept better this aspect of parenting.

Parents of fussy babies often feel a bit disappointed that they have been so blessed. They want to enjoy their babies but often don't. Their babies also want to feel right but don't. As a result, everyone is disappointed. Parents can resort to prayer, support, and counseling to help them adjust, but babies have no recourse but their parents.

Don't compare babies. A Christian mother of a high-need baby confided her feeling to me by saying, "Why can't I handle my baby? Other mothers seem more in control of their babies. They can leave them and get other things done; I can't." I advised this mother not to compare her baby with other babies. The other mothers may not share her views toward attachment parenting. High-need babies are not "better" or "worse" than other babies—just *different*. Besides, many people tend to exaggerate the goodness of their babies. Comparing babies contributes nothing to your relationship with your baby and may lead to frustration and burnout. It is common to have both easy and high-need babies in the same family. Our first three babies were relatively easy, our fourth was high-need. We had to "throw out the books" and start fresh—in fact, this baby inspired me to write a book on the subject—*The Fussy Baby*.

Don't Let Your Baby Cry

One of the most common dilemmas of parents, especially parents of fussy babies, is whether or not to let their babies cry. This problem is thoroughly explained in Chapter 2, but the following will remind you of a few points.

Young babies do not cry to annoy, to manipulate, or to take advantage of their parents. They cry because they have needs. To ignore their cries is to ignore their needs.

A fussy baby is endowed with a high-need level and a low stimulus barrier. Trust in his environment is one of the prime determinants of his eventual personality. An infant who does not receive a predictable response to his signals soon learns not to trust his signals and sometimes not to trust his caregivers. He eventually becomes less motivated to cry and will stop, but at what expense to his self-esteem? In this situation, a high-need baby completely resigns himself to a lower level of care.

Yes, babies are adaptable and resilient. Praise the Lord for having made them so; otherwise neither babies nor parents would survive child rearing. Yet babies whose cries fall upon deaf ears turn their outward anxieties inward and may experience behavior problems later on. Because they experience nonresponse as anger-producing (whereas response is experienced as love), they become angry babies and even angrier children.

Gentle Your Fussy Baby

Most fussy babies are calmed by two actions: motion and physical contact. One of the earliest forms of behavior modifications is called the "principle of competing behavior." By gentling your fussy baby you treat your baby's tense behavior with your gentle behavior. To comfort the fussy baby is to determine what type of motion and physical contact she likes and needs and how much you can give of yourself without exhausting your parental reserves.

You should experiment to find out what comforts your baby the most. Most babies prefer bare skin-to-skin contact. Some babies need almost constant stroking and patting, and they enjoy being left undressed. Other babies enjoy the security of being swaddled and held firmly. Experiment with which position she likes to be held: bent over your shoulder; up on your chest; flat over your knee, directly in front of you with one hand on her back and the other hand on her bottom so that she stares directly into your eyes while you sing to her and move rhythmically; or draped (stomach down) over your arm, her diaper nestled snugly in the bend of your arm.

After a while you will develop your own type of "colic carry." A winning combination for our family was for me to hold our baby firmly, chest against chest, with her head turned to one side and nestled under my chin, while I swayed rhythmically from side to side.

The combination of skin-to-skin contact, the baby's ear over your heart, your breathing movements, and your total body rhythm often will soothe a fussy baby. A mechanical baby swing can be useful, but be careful not to overuse it and let it become a parent substitute.

During the first few months of comforting your fussy baby, you may log many miles of walking, rocking, floor pacing, dancing, pram pushing, and so on. When all else fails, place your baby in a car seat and take a ride. This usually works. Baby carriers are ideal for calming a fussy baby, especially the sling-type carrier in which you can hold your baby facing forward and bent at the hips, which helps relax his tense abdomen. Within a few exhausting weeks or months, your baby will have told you what mode of transportation he likes best. Another "soother" is a sound and rhythm that mimics mother's heartbeat, something he was accustomed to *in utero*, such as a metronome set at seventy-five beats per minute, a record of a heartbeat, or the ticktock of a clock.

Relax

A fussy baby can shatter the nerves of even the most shatterproof mother. Relax by whatever method works. Being held in tense arms may upset a baby who is already sensitive to tense vibrations. This is called "tense mother–tense baby syndrome." Here are some relaxation tips.

1. *Take a warm bath* with your baby. Recline in the bathtub and fill the tub to just below breast level. Let your baby partially float while he is nursing; this ritual may soothe you both.

2. *Get outdoor exercise.* A relaxing walk in the park with your baby in a front carrier can be a daily ritual for a tense mother and fussy baby.

3. *Breastfeeding will usually soothe a fussy baby,* but sometimes even that doesn't work. If your baby refuses your breast and does not stop fussing, your baby may be signaling that he wants to lie down with you in bed and nurse tummy to tummy snuggled in your arms and breasts. In our family this has been a successful technique.

4. *Nap when your baby naps.* Sometimes when your baby sleeps, take the phone off the hook and have a private relaxing time doing something just for yourself. Spending time in the reading of God's Word is a real lift. All give and no take wears thin after a while, even for the most caring and giving Christian parent.

Plan Ahead

Scheduling is usually a bad word in baby care, but as many parents of fussy babies will tell you, the end sometimes justifies the means. Most babies have their best and their worst times of day, although being inconsistently appeased (what works one day does not work the next) is one of the hallmarks of a fussy baby. Most babies have some pattern of daily fussiness. Plan ahead by using your baby's good time for fun activities and attention to your other children, to yourself, and to your spouse. Some mothers use these times to prepare the evening meal ahead of time. Most babies have their main fussy periods from 4:00 to 8:00 P.M. If you've accomplished most of your daily duties by this time, you can settle down during the fussy period and devote most of your energy to comforting your baby.

Lean on Your Support Groups

You may reach a point in caring for your fussy baby when you need more support than advice. Surround yourself with supportive people and avoid the advice of the "let your baby cry" and "you're getting too attached" philosophers. In order to get the most out of your support group you must honestly state your feelings. Parenting is a guilt-producing profession. Nearly all parents at some time have the feeling of "I am not doing a good job." If you have a low acceptance level of your baby's crying and have reached the end of your rope, say so.

Many sincere and caring mothers have had momentary thoughts of "I hate my baby," "I feel like I am being had." If you confide these normal feelings to other parents who have survived fussy babies, you will probably receive the following comments: "It's okay to have these feelings"; "You are not being taken advantage of"; "You are not spoiling him"; "You are doing the most important job in the world—raising a human being."

CHAPTER 5

THE FAMILY
OF A
FUSSY BABY

Having a fussy baby can become a problem for the whole family. Because you have been blessed with a high-need baby, you probably will expend so much energy comforting your baby that you have little energy left for the needs of your spouse or other children. It is difficult to be a loving spouse or parent when you are emotionally and physically drained by the end of the day.

This next statement is not going to sit well with many mothers: most Christian writers agree that God's order of priorities is God, marriage, children, job, and church. It is difficult for many devoted mothers to put their marriage relationship before their children, especially when they seem to have so many needs.

With prayer and consultation this should not be an either/or decision. Parenting a fussy baby is a family affair. Both parents must work together to convey love and comfort to their baby and to each other. The fussy baby demands shared parenting. If a mother finds she has no time left for her husband, she should look closely at what other things (besides the baby) take her time and then make some changes. Time with husband is more important than housework. It is easy for parents of a fussy baby to experience burnout early in their parenting profession and in their marriage. Wife, keep a few channels of your communication network open for your husband. Husband, be sensitive to your wife. The single best support system for a fussy baby is a healthy Christian marriage.

A Checklist for Possible Causes of Your Baby's Fussiness

Although most babies fuss primarily because of their own temperaments and not because of any physical problems, occasionally pain-producing illnesses or disturbing stimuli in a baby's environment account for their fussiness. Discovering these takes a lot of detective work by the baby's parents and a physical examination by his pediatrician. Some of the more common causes of pain or discomfort in young babies are listed here.

1. *Does your baby have a medical problem*—ear infection, throat infection, eye irritation, constipation, hernia, allergies, irritating rash, or gastroesophageal reflux (also called pediatric regurgitation syndrome, see p. 101 for description)?

2. *What about the mother's diet?* If your doctor finds your baby to be healthy and there is no apparent pressure or pain-producing illness that could account for his fussiness, he may be intolerant to a substance in your milk. Suspect a digestive problem when your baby's fussiness is the colicky type. The following items in your diet could cause your baby's fussiness (in order of frequency): (a) milk and milk products; (b) caffeine-

containing substances taken in excess—coffee, tea, colas, and chocolate, and some medicines; (c) gas-producing raw vegetables—broccoli, cabbage, onions, green peppers, and beans; (d) citrus fruits or juice; (e) eggs; (f) medicines; and (g) decongestants, cold remedies, and prenatal vitamins containing iron. *Anything* in your diet could be causing trouble. Consider wheat, corn, oats, nuts, shellfish, tomatoes. Keep a record of what you are eating to help track down the offending foods. If you suspect any of these offenders, eliminate the suspected allergens for a period of at least three weeks. Sometimes it is a combination of several.

3. *What about the baby's diet?* She may be allergic to dairy products or formula; consult your doctor about a less allergy-causing formula. Vitamins or fluoride may cause reactions in some children.

4. *Check for environmental irritants,* such as cigarette smoke, perfumes, hairsprays, cleaning products that give off a strong odor, or recurring noises.

5. *Is your baby hungry?* (See Chapter 6 for suggestions about baby's getting enough to eat.)

6. *Is your environment too busy?* Birth is a social event that often brings a long line of well-wishers into the home of tired parents and a baby who may not be ready to be a socialite. Some babies fuss because of overstimulation: too many sitters, loud noises on TV, overly excited older siblings. Surprisingly, some babies actually enjoy a busy environment and settle better when there is a lot of noise.

How to Avoid Having a Fussy Baby

How can you prevent your baby from becoming a fussy baby? Try these simple preventive measures near the time of birth to ease your baby's adjustment to his new world.

1. Get in harmony with your baby *in utero*. Some researchers in the field of fetal awareness suspect that a mother's emotions during pregnancy can affect the baby's personality. Continue this harmony into your birthing environment.

2. Consider if the hospital newborn-care policies that separate mothers and babies in the Western culture may contribute to the fussy baby problem. Contrast these policies with those of other cultures where the baby is born into the arms and breasts of her mother, is carried close to her chest while she is working, is fed on demand, and sleeps skin-to-skin with her until she shows signs of comfortable independence. Researchers who have studied this type of immersion mothering in other cultures have noted that these babies fuss far less and seem much more content than babies in Western cultures. Smoothing the transition from the intrauterine to postnatal environment helps lessen what is called "missing the womb."

3. Practice the principles of attachment parenting mentioned in the first book in this series, *So You're Going to Be a Parent*, (bonding at birth, rooming-in at the hospital, breastfeeding on demand, and immersion mothering postpartum). These practices give your baby a smooth welcome into his world. Although I am not sure that the parents have less fussy babies, I have observed that parents who practice the principles of getting the right start are able to respond intuitively to their baby's cues and cope more effectively with a fussy baby.

Advantages to Having a Fussy Baby

Are there any advantages to parenting a fussy baby? Your first impulse may be to answer, "Absolutely none. This isn't any blessing!" There are certain fringe benefits enjoyed by parents who have sought proper counsel and prayed their way through the first six months of raising a fussy baby.

Their most impressive benefit is that they know their child. Their radar systems have been so intensely tuned into their child that they intuitively sense their baby's needs and respond to them.

Because they have been blessed with a baby with high-need levels, their acceptance and intuition (by constant usage) have matured to a higher level.

Because these parents know their child and have learned to anticipate their baby's behavior, they are better able to discipline their child when he or she is two and three years old. They always seem to be ahead of their child. Parenting a fussy baby is similar to parenting a child with a physical handicap or a painful illness. It brings out the best in intuitive parenting.

A fussy baby can actually bring a couple closer to God and closer to each other through prayer and consultation. Parents who have relied upon Scripture as their cope book learn a vital lesson that raises their entire parenting career to a spiritual level. They have asked God into their homes early in life.

These children are above average from the time of their birth. They need above-average parenting at home and above-average teaching in school. They will tax the ingenuity of teachers just as they do their parents. Give them above-average input, and you will be rewarded by children who are probably very intelligent and creative and who will bring joy to you and service to God.

Words of Comfort

"If my baby is fussy, is this an indication of what he will be like when he gets older? Will he be a hyperactive child?" The eventual behavior patterns of fussy babies vary from child to child. Some babies will fuss for their first six months and then settle down to become smooth and quiet children. Other babies who start out being a handful in early infancy often will remain a handful throughout childhood.

One day after counseling mothers of fussy babies, tired mothers, and mothers who were barely coping, I thought, *God must surely be reserving a special place for mothers*. I began to imagine what God says to mothers, and I wish to share these thoughts with you.

And God said to the mother . . .

When you were so tired that you thought you could not cope with your fussy baby another minute, I watched you; I was with you and you coped.

When you questioned My matching program for mothers and children, when you asked, "Lord, why have You given me such a difficult child when my friends have such easy babies?" I said, "Trust in Me with all your heart and lean not on your own understanding. I will not give you a cross you cannot bear."

When you prayed, thanking Me for a gifted child, I replied, "To whom much has been given much is expected."

When you felt the need to escape, you asked for help and I strengthened you.

When you were angry at your child's defiance, when you nearly lost control, you consulted Me and I guided your hand.

When you chastened your child instead of going too quickly to the rod, I saw your perseverance and this incident did not go unrecorded.

When you listened to your baby's nighttime needs, you pleaded, "Lord, I'm exhausted; if only I could get one full night's sleep I could go on." I heard your plea. I was awake with you. I gave you strength and you went on.

When you doubted your worth as a person, I listened. You and your child are precious in My sight. I reminded you that you are doing the most important job in the world, raising My child whom I have given you on short-term loan to nurture and return to Me. You have trained your child in the way he should go, and he has gone the way he should go. Come into My kingdom for I have reserved a special place for you.

How to Avoid Mother Burnout

"I feel trapped"; "I can't cope, but I have to"; "I can't handle this any longer"; "I'm not enjoying motherhood"; "God, I feel so guilty." These are quotes from Christian mothers who have shared their mothering difficulties and feel they are burning out.

What Is Burnout?

Burnout is a syndrome of signs and symptoms very much like postpartum depression. It is due to a total exhaustion of a mother's reserves and an increasing lack of fulfillment in the mothering profession. Burnout also stems from a chronic disenchantment, a feeling that motherhood is not all it is cracked up to be. In fact, some mothers think they are cracking up just being mothers. Throughout Scripture, children are presented as being a joy to parents, not a burden. Burnout implies that there has been some fundamental breakdown in God's design for the joy in the parent-child relationship.

What Causes Mother Burnout?

I think the most common cause of mother burnout is the *aloneness* that plagues today's mothers. Never before in history have mothers been required or expected to do so much for so many with so little support. Today's society is caught up in the supermom myth. Shortly after giving birth, the new mother is expected to resume her previous roles as impeccable housekeeper, loving and giving wife, gourmet cook, gracious hostess, and contributor to the family income. Few mothers today are allowed the luxury in the first few weeks after birth of following God's design— mothering as a first priority and all else following when time and energy permit. Today's women often enter motherhood with confusing role models, inadequate prenatal preparation, unrealistic expectations of what babies are like, and no coping skill to handle the babies they get.

How Can You Avoid Burnout?

Since one of my ministries is to advocate attachment parenting, I also have an interest in what happens when God's design is not followed. Throughout this book I mention the law of supply and demand as being part of God's plan. By that I mean that God will supply to both mother and father the energy to meet the demands of their child as long as the conditions are met that allow God's design for attachment parenting to operate. In my experience, when I look into cases of mother burnout, I can usually pinpoint one or more steps in the attachment style of parenting in which God's design was not followed; usually too many demands are placed on the mother that divert her energy away from her baby, or the mother is not allowed to operate in a supportive environment that allows her intuitive mothering to flourish.

Besides dispelling the supermom myth, I would like to correct the assumption that the baby is to blame for mother burnout. It is true that a high-need baby places a strain on the mother. However, if each situation is examined carefully, some interfering influence is detectable that has thrown off God's law of supply and demand, and the mother is not supplied with the energy she needs to cope with her high-need baby.

Mothers who have experienced burnout shouldn't feel guilty or feel they are not good mothers. In fact burnout is more likely to occur in highly motivated mothers. Mothers who strive to be perfect mothers or who want to fill all the roles are most likely to burn out. Also mothers who are attracted to this attachment parenting are candidates for burnout. A person first has to be on fire in order to be burned out.

71

The following checklist may help mothers avoid burnout. Mother, can you identify any risk factors you may have that predispose you to mother burnout?

1. Do you have a history of difficulty coping with combined stress?
2. During your pregnancy, did you have ambivalent feelings about how your child would interfere with your current lifestyle?
3. Were you involved in a high-recognition career before you became a mother?
4. Did you have poor mothering role models from your own mother?
5. Did you make adequate prenatal preparation, or did you have unrealistic expectations about how easy it is to care for babies?
6. Did you have labor and delivery in which fear and pain predominated, a generally negative birthing experience that was not what you expected?
7. Did you not have a bonding relationship shortly after birth?
8. Is yours a high-need baby?
9. Is there a mismatch of temperaments—you have a high-need baby, but you have a low level of acceptance?
10. Did you have marital disharmony, and did you hope that a baby might solve your marital problems?
11. Does your baby have an uninvolved father?
12. Are you highly motivated and compulsive? Do you strive to be the perfect mother?
13. Are you an overcommitted mother with too many outside priorities?

14. Have there been too many changes too fast, such as moving, extensive remodeling, or redecorating, to upset your nesting instinct?
15. Is there a medical illness in mother, father, or baby?
16. Do you have financial pressures?
17. Are you becoming confused by conflicting parenting advice?
18. Have you had too many babies too soon, that is, less than two years apart?

Mother burnout is usually the result of a combination of several of these factors, which, put together, have a cumulative effect.

Recognize Early Warning Signs of Burnout

When I see a mother who has several risk factors, I place a red star at the top of her baby's chart, signifying a red alert that this mother is subject to burning out unless preventive medicine is administered. I urge pastors, friends, relatives, and health care professionals to be on the lookout for these red flags. Some early warning signs of impending burnout include:

1. *"I don't enjoy my child."* Not enjoying your child means that you are not in harmony with your child.

2. *"I'm not a good mother."* Realize that because you love your child so deeply, these feelings of shaky confidence are normal. The more you love and care for another person, the more vulnerable you are to your own feelings of inadequacy. What is not normal is the persistence of these feelings to the point that you do not enjoy your mothering and you begin to search for alternative forms of self-fulfillment.

73

3. *"I don't feel right with God."* Many mothers have shared with me that they have the most difficulty being in harmony with their children when they're not in harmony with God.

4. *"I can't sleep."* If you're not in harmony with your baby at night, you have a greater chance of being burned out during the day. (See Chapter 8 for suggestions on achieving nighttime harmony.)

Survival Tips for the Burned-Out Mother

Have Realistic Expectations

Realistically prepare yourself during your pregnancy. Become involved in support groups that help you develop realistic expectations of what babies are like. Many parents do not realize that a new baby absolutely will dominate their lives and completely change their previously predictable and organized schedules. A common complaint I hear when tired couples come for their babies' two-week checkup is "Nobody prepared me for this."

Encourage Father Involvement

I have never seen a case of mother burnout in a home in which the father "mothered" the mother and created an atmosphere in the home that allowed God's design of attachment parenting to flourish. In most homes suffering from mother burnout, the mothers did not recognize the signs of burnout and did not call for help, and the fathers were insensitive to their wives' impending trouble.

Father, be sensitive to these early warning signs and

risk factors. Don't wait for your wife to tell you she is burning out, since wives do not usually confide these ambivalent feelings to their husbands, perhaps because they do not want to shatter their perfect-mother image. As one exhausted mother complained to me, "I'd have to pass out in front of my husband before he would realize how tired I really am."

Burnout is common in homes in which there is what I call the "misattachment syndrome." In this situation, the parents are usually blessed with a high-need child. Mother immerses herself into meeting the needs of this demanding child and tries her best to mother according to God's design. Father, on the other hand, because he feels a bit shaky handling a fussy baby and also feels his wife is becoming too attached, often withdraws and retreats to interests away from home that he can control more easily.

A high-need child, a burning-out mother, and a withdrawing father make up the highest potential for a total family burnout. It has the highest potential for a marriage burnout. When mother becomes overly attached to her baby, father may form outside attachments of his own, and the whole family eventually may become detached because God's design for this support system was not followed.

Father, be sensitive to your wife's burnout signs and give her the message, "I'll take over, you do something just for yourself." One of my favorite stories illustrates this point. One day a noninvolved father sent his burning-out wife into my office for some counseling, which gave the subtle message, "It must be her fault we have a demanding kid she can't handle." Since it was the father who sent the mother in, I thought it was my professional duty to prescribe the medicine that got right to the heart of the problem. I gave the mother a prescription and said, "Now, be sure you husband fills this prescription for you." The prescription read, "Administer one dose of a caring husband and involved father three times a day and before bedtime until symptoms subside."

How does the father benefit from becoming more involved? A burned-out mother soon becomes a burned-out wife, and the entire marriage relationship suffers. Quite honestly, by supporting your wife according to God's design in the early months of mothering, you will reap rewards beyond your greatest expectations. The mother-father roles are not as well-defined in today's society as they have been in the past. Because of the breakdown of the extended family, today's mothers feel alone. The father needs to make up for this aloneness and become the mother's most reliable support system.

Mother, tell your husband what you need. A mother often is unwilling to release her child or to be assertive asking her husband to take over some of their child's care. But this harmony and mutual sensitivity are vitally important for the Christian family to survive in today's society. I advise you to sit down periodically and write an "I need help" list. Tell your husband exactly where and how you need help. A sensitive husband also can relieve the pressure on his wife by saying that he doesn't expect the house to look as it did before the child's arrival.

Practice Attachment Parenting, Not Restraint Parenting

Attachment parenting, if given the time and the commitment to develop, helps you develop harmony with your baby, increases your perseverance level, helps you know and have more realistic expectations of your baby's behavior, and generally helps you enjoy your baby more. Enjoying your baby is emphasized because it seems to have a snowballing effect on your acceptance level and your self-confidence. Restraint parenting, on the other hand, ultimately leads to chronic disenchantment with the whole parenting role.

A common error in advice to mothers facing burnout is encouraging restraint parenting. It may work for some mother-child relationships, but in my experience, it is a short-term gain for a long-term loss. It is usually not separation from the child that the mother needs; it is a complete overhaul of her support system to minimize the competing influences that drain her energy. She also needs to consider other factors that may boost her self-esteem.

Know Your Tolerance Levels

Just as there is wide variation in temperaments of babies, there is wide variation in the tolerance levels of mothers. Some mothers seem to have high-acceptance levels that allow them to mother a dozen kids and function like human gymnasiums all day long. Other mothers have lower acceptance levels and have more difficulty coping with the constant demands of too many children too soon, especially in the toddler age group. As one mother of a newborn and a two year old put it, "I feel like I'm still pregnant with our two year old."

If you already have a high-need baby and are having difficulty coping, you would be wise to consider spacing your children at least three years apart. Many mothers let themselves operate on their energy reserves too long before seeking help. If you find your tolerance level is nearing its saturation point, seek counseling now. A Christian counselor can help you and your husband have realistic expectations of your God-given acceptance level. Then you can make some necessary changes in the family situation that you can tolerate more realistically.

A graphic example of this acceptance-level problem was conveyed to me by a mother of a high-need child. She was frustrated by apparently not measuring up to all that was expected of her: "My life is a circle revolving around my child. But I need a square with some edges left just for me." During my years as a pediatrician, I have been impressed by the way so many mothers can cope with so many combined stresses for so long.

Define Priorities

The earlier you realize you cannot be all things to all people and still have enough energy left for yourself and your baby, the less risk you have of burning out. Sometimes it's necessary to sit down, make a list of all the daily activities draining your energy, and put them in the order of priority. This is a good time for a family council during which a mother defines realistically what she has to do and what she is able to do, and the father and older children define daily chores they can do. Then the family prays together for God's perspective and guidance in accomplishing this.

Mother's of high-need children often say, "But I get nothing done." You *are* getting something done, something important. You just don't receive the gratification of seeing instant results. For example, an exhausted mother of a high-need child recently shared with me that her most competing energy drain was her compulsive housekeeping habits. But one day she looked at the floor and exclaimed, "That floor doesn't have feeling. No one's life is going to be affected if that floor is not scrubbed every day. My baby is a baby for a very short time, and she has feeling." A wise mother determines just what *needs* to be done.

Save Energy for Yourself

Some mothers may feel honestly they cannot be satisfied by one role. Babies are takers and mothers are givers, but there will come times when mothers feel all given out. It is often necessary for a caring third party, preferably the father, to step into this mother-infant relationship and encourage the mother to take better care of herself so she can take better care of the baby. If a mother is allowed to burn out and continues to practice martyr-mothering against her will, eventually the whole family will burn out and nobody will win.

Part 2

Your Baby's Physical Needs

CHAPTER 6

WEANING, SOLID FOODS, AND OTHER DIETARY CONCERNS

I do not recommend early weaning for infants. I firmly believe that the custom of early weaning in Western society is not in accordance with God's design for mother-infant attachment. Weaning an infant before his time is an unfortunate break in the nurturing continuum. Women of the Western world are accustomed to considering breastfeeding in terms of months. When a mother asks me how long she should nurse her baby, I respond, "There is no set number of *years* you should nurse your baby."

There are many "weanings" throughout a child's life—weaning from the womb, from the breast, from home to school, and from authority at home. The pace at which children go from oneness to separateness should be respected in all of these weaning milestones. To hurry a child through any of these relationships may show disrespect for the child's dignity as a little person with big needs. La Leche League's term for nursing toddlers, *little nursing persons*, certainly demonstrates this respect.

The Dos and Don'ts of Weaning

A basic principle of child care to remember is that as your child grows older, her needs do not lessen, they only change. *The American Heritage Dictionary* defines *weaning:* "to withhold mother's milk and substitute other nourishment." There are two phases in weaning: detachment and substitution. As a baby is detached from the nutritional nourishment of mother's milk and solid food is substituted for it, other forms of emotional nourishment also should be substituted for the emotional detachment from mother's breast.

There are some definite dos and don'ts for mothers in weaning.

1. *Don't wean by leaving your child abruptly.* Except in unavoidable tragic situations, weaning by desertion is definitely to be avoided. Detachment from a mother's breast and detachment from the mother herself may be a combined stress that is too much for the baby to handle.

2. *Practice the "don't offer, don't refuse" technique* advocated by the La Leche League. Your baby probably will start to skip one feeding time a day because he is busy with other pursuits. After several weeks of skipping this nursing, you may find he will be equally willing to miss another feeding. As the weeks and months pass, he may be nursing only when he needs to fall asleep for naps and bedtime. Be prepared to allow him to retreat a bit (or a lot) during times of stress such as illness, new developmental stages, changes in environment, and so on. You may be willing, even eager, to continue this "put me to sleep" nursing for quite a while longer. If there is a definite reason, however, that

you need to encourage an end to this, be careful to consider your baby's needs too. There is no shortcut in this process—you are still committed to filling your little one's needs, one way or another. If you must discontinue the bedtime nursing, try substituting stories and a cuddle, but you may have to cuddle in positions other than the familiar nursing position. Let your husband take over at these times if possible, and spend more one-on-one time together throughout the day to reassure your child of your availability and commitment. (See the Bibliography for good books on nursing your toddler.)

3. *Don't set up an arbitrary date at which you are going to wean.* As in many aspects of child rearing, the clock and the calendar have no place in the breastfeeding relationship. You probably will feel different about your goal as the preordained time approaches.

Breast-fed babies do not need vitamin supplements. If your nutrition is adequate, your milk contains all the necessary vitamins and nutrients your infant will need for her first six to nine months.

The Biblical Approach to Weaning

Weaning took place very late among the Israelites, at least by today's standards. Hebrew mothers often suckled their children for three years. Weaning was a festive occasion, not a feeling of loss or detachment: "Abraham made a great feast on the same day that Isaac was weaned" (Gen. 21:8). The peace and contentment a child should have by the time he is weaned is stated beautifully in Psalm 131:2.

Surely I have calmed and quieted my soul,
Like a weaned child with his mother;
Like a weaned child is my soul within me.

A beautiful commentary on the meaning of this psalm is given in Lang's *Commentary on the Holy Scriptures.*

As the weaned child no longer cries, frets, and longs for the breast, but lies still and is content because it is with its mother; so my soul is weaned from all discontented thoughts, from all fretful desires for earthly good, waiting in stillness upon God, finding its satisfaction in His presence, resting peacefully in His arms.

The term *weaning* takes on a new connotation in 1 Kings 11:20: "Then the sister of Tahpenes bore him Genubath his son, whom Tahpenes weaned in Pharaoh's house." *Weaned* is used here to mean educating or bringing up the child. The NIV translation is "whom Tahpenes brought up."

The biblical story of Hannah and her son Samuel is an early account of mother-infant attachment and priority mothering:

Now the man Elkanah and all his house went up to offer to the LORD the yearly sacrifice and his vow. But Hannah did not go up, for she said to her husband, "Not until the child is weaned; then I will take him, that he may appear before the LORD and remain there forever." So Elkanah her husband said to her, "Do what seems best to you; wait until you have weaned him. . . ." Then the woman stayed and nursed her son until she had weaned him. (1 Sam. 1:21–23)

Verse 24 describes the sacrifice Hannah offered when Samuel was dedicated to the Lord.

I regard Hannah's weaning Samuel as an example of God's design for weaning a child from his mother to his God. Bible commentators feel that Samuel's weaning occurred when he was three years of age. "Do what seems best to you" is a clear indication that Elkanah supported Hannah's God-given intuition.

Mothers, meditate on these scriptural passages, asking God to instill in you their meaning and the way in which they may be applied to your own mother-child relationship. I wish to share with you my own understanding of these passages. The Hebrew word for *weaned* in the above passages is *gamal*, which means "to ripen." The term implies a state of readiness. Weaning should not mean a loss or a detachment from a relationship but rather a state in which a child feels so full and so right that he is ready to take on other relationships. Weaning implies a smooth continuum from the security and instruction from his mother to the security and instruction from God. Weaning before his time of spiritual readiness may leave a child unfulfilled and just not feeling right. Perhaps a child who is weaned before his time from any childhood relationship and is hurried into other relationships may rebel both inwardly and outwardly and show what I call "diseases of unreadiness." My pediatrician's intuition tells me what are considered normal behaviors of infancy and childhood, such as aggression, tantrum-like behavior, and severe mood swings (all forms of baby-anger), may in fact be diseases of premature weaning.

Breastfeeding is for both nutritional and emotional nourishment. I would advise you to breastfeed your infant for nutrition at least *one year*. Many infants who are weaned before their time experience medical illnesses shortly after weaning such as ear infections, diarrhea, and allergies. Breastfeed past the first year for emotional nourishment. A nursing toddler is a beautiful sight. I enjoy hearing the little "nursing conversations" from a two-and-a-half-year-old during breastfeeding, such as, "all done—close the door." In the second year, breastfeeding functions more as a securing lift, a pick-me-up during times of stress, and a time mother and baby can relax and have their special dialogue. One of my two-year-old patients was in the office for a checkup. When she had finished nursing, she looked up at her mother and said, "Mommy's Moo. No caffeine, no sugar."

You may ask, "But, doctor, won't prolonged nursing make my baby too dependent on me?" The answer is an unreserved no! Most mothers who have nursed for several years have found their children actually to be more secure and more independent. Certainly in our own family this has been the case. Our four-year-old daughter, Hayden, enjoyed nursing until just after her fourth birthday and then willingly exclaimed, "I don't like it anymore." Martha was then pregnant with out daughter Erin, which accounts for the change in taste. Hayden then said, "I'll wait till the baby comes then the good milk will be back." Five months later she just wasn't interested anymore. Again, the age at which a baby evolves from oneness to separateness should be respected for each individual mother-infant couple.

"How Long Should My Baby Be on Formula?"

Keep your baby on formula for at least one year. If you are breastfeeding and choose to wean your infant within a year, wean to formula and not to cow's milk. Each species' milk is its ideal food (human milk for humans); it is not the ideal food when it crosses species (cow's milk for humans). Babies fed cow's milk before they are one year of age often have intestinal disturbances such as allergies and anemia, low iron in the blood. Since most formulas are basically cow's milk that has been modified for babies, formula gives babies the nutritional advantages of cow's milk without the problems of drinking it straight.

Generally, I advise mothers to keep their babies on formula until they lose the taste for it. If your pediatrician feels your baby is gaining too much weight on the usual formula (twenty calories per ounce), he or she may suggest you feed him a lower-calorie formula. Low-calorie formula is an attempted imitation of human milk, which naturally decreases in calories as your infant grows older because he needs fewer calories per pound of body weight. Switching from formula to cow's milk is often done for psychological rather than nutritional reasons, since this switch may be considered an index of the baby's "growing up." Thinking of your baby's formula as actual "milk" may help you overcome this temptation.

After deciding to switch from formula to cow's milk, you must decide what kind of cow's milk to feed your baby. Milk differs in fat content and, therefore, calorie content. Pediatricians advise against the use of skim milk before a baby is two years old since this lower-calorie milk deprives the infant of the valuable energy source and essential fatty acids and because it contains more salt and protein than a baby's immature kidneys can handle. If your baby is overweight on whole milk, 2 percent milk is a safe alternative. If your baby is not overweight and is not a compulsive milk drinker, then use whole milk.

Introducing Solid Foods— When, What, and How Much?

Solid food is for the mature (see Heb. 5:14). Most infants under six months of age do not need solid food. However, your baby may show signs after he is four months old that indicate he is willing and ready to take solid foods.

Your baby's interval between milk feedings gets shorter and shorter, and your intuition tells you he is less satisfied even after three or four days of increased nursing. Solids are usually given to breast-fed infants later because breastfeeding mothers respond to a growth spurt by increasing the frequency of feedings for several days until the supply equals the new demand level. Bottle-feeding mothers are more likely to want to begin solids than increase the number of formula feedings since they are more in the habit of counting bottles than breastfeeding mothers are in counting nursings. The nutritional needs of most infants can be met fully by breastfeeding or by an iron-fortified formula alone for nine months.

Your baby's need to chew and bite becomes obvious when she starts to teethe, which is usually around six months. Her tongue and mouth muscles are ready for the new skill of taking in solid food and swallowing it. She watches you eat with great interest, and since the best way to explore any unknown is to grab it and put it in her mouth, that's what she tries to do with the food she sees you eating. When you find yourself competing with your baby for your own dinner, the time is right to let her discover this new way of eating. If she is in a highchair or on your lap, simply offer her a tiny taste on the tip of your finger. She will grab your finger and eagerly suck on it to experience this new material. If you use a spoon, fill just the very tip of it, because she will grab the spoon (be prepared for a mess). Your baby may get a pleased and excited expression on her face, or she may frown and let the offered food slide right back out. Most babies like ripe, mashed bananas or yellow vegetables, like squash or sweet potatoes, or rice cereal mixed with a little breast milk or water. Mashed bananas and small amounts of soft rice cereal are good test foods for solid feeding because they are most like milk in taste and texture.

Babies have naturally built-in protective mechanisms that push unpleasant objects out with their tongues. They have to outgrow this tongue-thrust reflex before they are ready for solid foods. If your baby eagerly and easily swallows her first dose, then she has demonstrated her readiness. If the banana comes back at you rather quickly or if your baby demonstrates difficulty in swallowing or a lack of desire, then she is not ready.

Introducing solid food is much easier when your baby has the maturity to handle the eating process: reaching out and touching food, sitting up with support, and "mouthing" the food. Babies usually show these signs of readiness by six months.

Infant feeders (or nipples with extra large holes)

that allow babies to suck baby food through a nipple are not acceptable. Babies should learn to use different muscle actions for solid foods than suck-swallow. A baby who is too young to use the correct eating muscles is too young to be given solid food. If it is the mess you are worried about, here is a hint for less messy feeding times: put baby in a high chair facing you and gently hold his hands in your nondominant hand while you feed him with your other hand. Older babies should be allowed to feed themselves as much as possible with their hands. The goal here is not how much food you can shovel in but how well baby learns to explore and enjoy his food.

Feed solid food after your baby's bottle. Milk should be your baby's primary nutrition during the first nine months since it is the most complete source of balanced nutrition. Solid foods should complement the milk feedings, not interfere with them. The interval between the bottle and the solid food is a matter of your convenience.

Since infants have no concept of breakfast, lunch, and dinner food, it really makes no difference whether they get fruit for breakfast or for dinner. Morning is usually the best time to offer solid foods to formula-fed infants because it is usually the time of day when mothers have the most time to prepare their infants' food. Breast-fed infants should be offered solids when their milk supply is lowest, usually toward the end of the day. Begin with a small amount of solid food (possibly a quarter teaspoon) since your initial goal is to introduce your baby gradually to a variety of foods, not to fill him up. The following suggestions on when and what kind of solid foods to introduce are only general guidelines and should be modified to fit your baby's specific needs and desires.

Fruits

Fruits are about 96 percent carbohydrates and, therefore, are not a good source of balanced nutrition. Avocados are an exception in that they contain a good percentage of polyunsaturated fat (the healthy kind), which makes this fruit a good early food for babies. One of the main benefits of fruits is that they mix well with other foods and can be used to increase the acceptance of more nutritious but less palatable foods. For example, your baby may take cereal more readily if it is covered with bananas. First introduce the fruits that are less allergenic and that have less citric acid, such as bananas, pears, and apples. Bananas are a good first food. Ripe, mashed bananas are accepted by most babies because they are sweet, have a smooth consistency, and closely resemble milk. I do not usually recommend strawberries, since many babies have an allergic reaction to them.

Juice

I do not recommend offering infants less than a year old large volumes of fruit juice. Undiluted fruit juice is almost as high in calories as milk but is much less nutritious, and juice is less advantageous than the fruit itself because the pulp has been removed. Because juice is less filling than milk, infants often take lots of juice without feeling full. The consumption of large quantities of juice is a subtle cause of childhood obesity in some infants. Also, excessive juice can cause diarrhea. For these reasons, I recommend diluting juice with an equal quantity of water, especially for the compulsive juice drinker. To avoid juice-bottle cavities (dental cavities resulting from giving a baby a bottle of fruit juice at naptime), dentists recommend that feeding a baby juice be delayed until he can drink from a cup.

Cereal

Cereal, like bananas, is one of the first solid foods a baby readily accepts because its consistency is closer to milk than that of many other solid foods. Cereal is often used as a filler to lengthen a baby's intervals between bottles or to encourage him to sleep through the night. This filler-food concept usually does not work, and it may contribute to obesity if overused. A baby is more comfortable when fed small amounts of solid foods frequently. (Feeding involves more than just physical nourishment and nutrition; both the parent and child should enjoy this feeding relationship.) If you are an exhausted mother who is not enjoying the feeding relationship because you have to feed your baby too often, especially at night, then using cereal for filler certainly should not be discouraged. Begin with rice or barley cereal, which are the least allergenic. Avoid mixed cereals until your baby has experienced each cereal made with those grains and has proved to not be allergic to them. Begin with a teaspoon of rice cereal and mix it with formula or breast milk to the desired and acceptable consistency. Adding fruits such as bananas or pears to the cereal may overcome its blandness and increase your baby's acceptance of it. Never force-feed your baby since this introduces a negative experience into his early eating habits. When a baby is satisfied he will turn his head away or refuse the foods.

Meats

Meat is an excellent source of iron and protein. Meats and iron-fortified cereals are the prime sources of iron for infants who do not receive vitamin-fortified formulas. Avoid purchasing meat dinners or meat mixtures. The protein and iron content of these mixtures is lower than that of plain meat since these mixtures are very high in starch. Liver and beef are the meats that are highest in iron, but they may not be accepted as easily by your infant as lamb, poultry, and veal.

Vegetables

Vegetables are a good source of carbohydrates and protein. The yellow vegetables, such as squash and carrots, are usually accepted better by young infants because of their taste and consistency. In theory, vegetables should be introduced before fruits since they are a much better source of balanced nutrition than fruits; however, because of fruits' sweetness, infants usually accept them better than vegetables.

Egg Yolks

Egg yolks are a good source of protein and fat. Although egg yolks are rich in iron, the kind of iron contained in them may not be absorbed easily by human intestines. A baby may be given a cooked egg yolk any time after she is six months old, and one egg yolk every other day is sufficient. Delay feeding her egg whites until she is a year old since egg whites tend to be more allergenic than yolks. If your baby is generally allergic or if you have a strong family history of allergies, delay introducing egg yolks or whites until she is at least one year of age.

95

Dairy Products

It is wise to avoid cow's milk as a beverage until your infant is at least one year of age because younger infants often do not tolerate cow's milk sugars or are allergic to cow's milk proteins. Some yogurts and cheeses, however, are tolerated better than milk because the allergenic products have been modified in the culturing process. Yogurt and cheese give all the nutritional benefits of milk without the potential problems and may be introduced into your infant's diet when he is about nine months old.

Give Your Infant a Balanced Diet

Giving your infant proper nutrition involves two basic requirements: the right amount of calories and the proper distribution of calories. Nutritionists have determined the proper distribution of calories by analyzing God's perfect nutrient—breast milk. The calories your infant consumes should be distributed in the following proportions: 30 to 45 percent fats, 35 to 50 percent carbohydrates, and 7 to 15 percent proteins. Your infant uses these calories for the following needs: 50 percent for his basic metabolism (the number of calories he needs simply to keep his body going), 30 percent for the energy he expends during activity, and 20 percent for continued growth. The percentage of calories he needs for growth is greatest during his first few months, 30 percent, and gradually decreases to 5 to 10 percent by one year of age. For this reason, the sooner nutritional deficiency occurs, the more it affects your infant's growth.

Breast milk and formula contain the appropriate proportions of carbohydrates, fats, and proteins. By one year of age, most infants receive about 50 percent of their nutrients from solid food. Between the ages of six months and a year, most infants need twenty-five to thirty-two ounces of formula per day, depending on the amount of solid food they are eating.

Your goal is to balance the proportions of carbohydrates, fats, and proteins in your infant's solid feedings as you have in her milk. A one-year-old baby who consumes about twenty ounces of formula a day and a large amount of fruits and fruit juices but refuses other food has a nutritional deficiency since the calories she receives are almost all carbohydrates, no fats, and no proteins. Another infant consumes about forty ounces of formula per day but simply refuses solid foods. If he is receiving the proper iron-fortified formula, then probably no nutritional deficiency exists. This baby has chosen to retain milk as his prime source of nutrition and has a balanced diet. A baby who consumes a variety of solid foods (four ounces of meat, vegetables, fruits, cereals, and egg yolk) and only takes eight to ten ounces of milk a day also has a balanced diet but has chosen a feeding pattern based predominantly on solid foods. As long as your baby is receiving a proper supply and distribution of nutrients, the source is not important.

Adding solid foods to baby's diet will change the character of his bowel movements. The stool of breast-fed babies will lose the almost pleasant "ripe buttermilk" odor (one reason breastfeeding mothers hesitate to start solids). Some babies will get runny stools; other babies will get firmer stools. If your baby becomes constipated, see "Common Intestinal Problems" in Chapter 7.

How to Prepare
Your Own Baby Food

I am sympathetic to baby food industries that are trying to achieve the economically impossible by keeping quality up and costs down. They have tried to use additives to keep food from spoiling and make it more palatable, but parental pressure has prompted them to eliminate monosodium glutamate, sugar, salt, and other chemicals from baby food. This constant adding to and subtracting from baby food according to fluctuating pressures often leaves parents very confused when they read labels. The current labels emphasize more what foods do not contain than what they do contain.

A steady diet of convenience foods has no place in infant nutrition. Making your own baby food from fresh, lean meat and fresh, seasonal vegetables and fruit is nutritionally superior to commercially processed baby foods. The following tips can enable you to prepare your own baby food at home.

- You will need a blender, ice cube trays with individual one-ounce cube sections, small freezer bags, and a pinch of creativity. Puree the fresh foods (vegetables should be cooked by steaming rather than boiling to preserve the many nutrients) through the baby food grinder or blender and pour them into the ice cube tray; then freeze the entire tray full of cube-size baby food. After freezing, remove the cubes and store them in plastic bags. Each time a feeding is needed, simply thaw one of these frozen cubes by placing it in a dish in a pan of hot water and you will have instant, nutritious baby food.

- Liver is a very good source of iron that, when blended with cottage cheese, makes a creamy pâté that is very nutritious.

- Teething biscuits and nutritious cookies and crackers can be prepared from whole-grain recipes found in a number of cookbooks on the market. Wheat products should be delayed until at least one year of age.

- Your infant can drink the same fruit juice as the rest of the family, but dilute the juice about half and half with water.

- It is never necessary to add sugar, salt, or any artificial preservatives to any baby food made at home. Lemon juice is often recommended as a natural preservative.

At about nine months, finger foods become fun; and self-feeding is good for baby's fine motor development, even though he may make a humorous mess. The following ideas for finger foods are both appealing and safe: pieces of peeled fruit, cheese cubes, cooked carrot "wheels," tiny broccoli "trees," rice cakes, bits of cooked hamburger, flakes of tuna or cooked white fish (remove any tiny bones), or chicken legs with a little meat still attached (take the sliver bone off).

Feeding Your Toddler— The Picky Eater

"My baby won't eat" is a common complaint about the one to two year old, and periodic disinterest in foods earns the toddler the title of "picky eater." The normal eating behavior of your busy toddler has gone something like this. During his first year you grew accustomed to feeding him a lot because he grew a lot. However, his growth rate is not nearly as rapid during his second year; so, he eats less.

Feeding a toddler is a combination of basic nutrition and creative marketing. Here is a feeding tip more in keeping with the realistic expectations of toddler behavior: prepare a toddler nibble tray with nutritious bits of food—raisins, cheese cubes, whole wheat bread sticks or strips of toast, orange wedges, apple slices with peanut butter, slices of meat, broccoli trees, hard-boiled egg wedges, and so on. Place this well-displayed "rainbow lunch" on your toddler's table, a table from which he can eat at his own pace. You will notice that your toddler will cruise by the tray and nibble at least ten times a day as he makes his rounds around the house.

Sitting down at the table can be primarily a time for communication, and as your child grows older, it can be a time for cleaning his plate. The concept of nibbling between meals may not agree with some parents who are used to mealtime discipline and three square meals a day. However, there is a good medical reason for this suggestion; your child will have blood-sugar swings when he is hungry. This is why most children's behavior deteriorates in late morning and midafternoon or just before the next meal. The practice of nibbling consistently all day long prevents these blood-sugar swings and therefore may be beneficial for your toddler's behavior. Patternless eating is normal for your toddler. He may "eat well" one day and "eat nothing" the next. If you average out his intake throughout the week, you will be surprised how balanced his diet is. Be sure to provide the four basic food groups in your toddler's snack tray: (1) dairy products, (2) meat and poultry, (3) fruits and vegetables, and

(4) cereals and grains. Feeding a busy toddler brings out the best in creative mothering.

Feeding Problems

Spitting Up, Regurgitation

All babies spit up, but some babies spit up more than others. At what point does spitting up go from being just a nuisance to being something medically wrong? If your baby is gaining weight normally and looks happy and healthy, then spitting up is more a temporary nuisance than a prolonged medical problem. If your baby does not look well and is not thriving normally, then you should consult your doctor for further advice on why your baby is spitting up. Spitting up is usually caused by swallowing excessive air or food, by an allergy, or by a gastroesophageal reflux. Some babies spit up several times a day, and the volume of regurgitated milk always seems more than it really is. To lessen your baby's degree of regurgitation try the following suggestions.

1. Lessen air intake by properly burping your baby.
2. Offer a smaller volume of food more frequently, and burp your baby well during breastfeeding or halfway through a bottle.
3. Keep your baby in the upright position as long as you can after each feeding (at least twenty to thirty minutes). This technique is especially helpful for very young babies. In some tiny babies, the esophagus joins the stomach at less of an angle so that when the stomach contracts, milk is pushed back up into the esophagus and out the baby's mouth. As your baby gets older, this angle becomes greater

and most of this reflux subsides. Keeping your baby in the upright position after feedings allows gravity to hold the food down in the stomach and intestines, thus minimizing reflux. At night, you may be able to feed your baby in the lying down position without any trouble. But reflux is a major cause of night waking so it would be helpful to prop your baby upright against your body after the feeding to be sure he burps well and to give gravity time to settle the milk.

4. Keep your baby's nasal passages clear. A stuffy nose causes baby to breathe through his mouth, and mouth breathing aggravates air swallowing.

Spitting up usually subsides by six to eight months, at which time your baby is sitting up after feedings and gravity is keeping the food down. Thereafter, jostling or crawling after feedings may cause your baby to spit up temporarily.

The Colicky Baby

Colic is one of the most severe discomforts a baby can suffer during his first few months. His parents will need a lot of prayer and counsel to survive this period and will need a lot of parental intuition to comfort their unhappy baby. The typical colicky baby cries from an intense physical discomfort, draws his legs onto a tense, gas-filled abdomen, and clenches his fists as if he were angry about his uncontrollable pain. His parents feel equally helpless about alleviating his misery.

Colic has many causes, but this explanation is limited to the four most common causes: (1) excessive swallowing and retention of air, (2) milk allergy, (3) the pain-tension cycles in a hyperexcitable baby, (4) gastro-esophageal reflux.

Swallowing and retaining a lot of air is the most common cause of colic. Babies who suck ravenously swallow enormous amounts of air, thus calling upon parents to continue the ancient custom of "burping," "bubbling," or "winding" the baby. I have enjoyed watching the nurses on the pediatric wards at some hospitals where there is at least one "burping specialist" whose feeding expertise is equated with the ability to get the most milk in and the most wind out. If the air a baby swallows settles on top of the milk in her stomach, the air can be burped up and out and usually causes no discomfort to the baby. However, when this air settles beneath the milk in the stomach two problems can result: regurgitation (spitting up) and pain or colic. When the stomach—which is distended by both milk and air—contracts, the milk goes up and the air goes down. The swallowed air winds its way through the intestines, stretching them and producing pain. The crying infant instinctively draws up her legs to relax her abdomen and pass the air through her rectum to relieve her discomfort. If the milk is regurgitated, it may carry some stomach acids that cause a burning feeling in the baby's esophagus; this may be another source of pain.

Swallowing and trapping air also causes a common feeding problem, the persistently hungry baby. The swallowed air gives the baby a false sense of fullness in his stomach. The "full" baby falls asleep without taking much milk and seems satisfied, but as soon as the air passes, he wakes again, hungry for his next meal of milk and air.

There are several ways to comfort your colicky

baby. Minimize the air he swallows by burping early in his feedings and more often, especially if your baby is a ravenous drinker or "gulper." Try to eliminate the air swallowing before it becomes trapped in the stomach. If your baby is always ravenous he could benefit from more frequent feedings so that he does not have the starved, anxious look, driven to suck too vigorously and gulp a lot of air. If he waits too long between feedings, try waking him sooner, not waiting till he's screaming to take a cue that he's hungry. If you are bottle-feeding, be sure the nipple's hole is large enough for milk to pass through it freely. If the holes are too small, your baby will have to suck more vigorously to obtain milk and consequently will swallow more air. Milk should drip out at a rate of at least one drop per second from a full bottle held upside down and not shaken. If the hole seems too small, take a small sewing needle and insert it eye-end into a cork and heat the needle on a stove burner until it is red hot. Poke a hole in the nipple large enough to see through. Collapsible plastic bags that fit into a bottle holder also may lessen air intake.

Colic does occur in breast-fed babies, but not as often. The human nipple has many holes that allow milk to flow according to the vigor of the baby's suck. These nipple holes also have a valve-like action that stops the spurt of milk when the baby stops sucking. If the mother's breast is quite full at the start of a feeding, her milk-ejection reflex will cause milk to spray out forcefully even if her baby stops sucking, causing him to swallow air. It may help for the mother to express some milk before starting to nurse, or let the gush of milk spend itself in a towel.

Some babies do not burp easily, and some babies

need to burp more frequently than others. If your baby does not spit up persistently or suffer from significant colic, then your burping techniques are certainly adequate for your individual baby. If your baby does not burp well and your instinct tells you there is a trapped bubble of air in her tummy, try shifting her position— lay her over your lap on her stomach or on her right side to burp her. This allows the trapped bubble of air to rise to the top of her stomach. After a few minutes, hold her sitting upright, leaning forward against your hand, and pat her back firmly to allow her to burp. A stubborn bubble often comes up after you've changed your baby's diaper and lifted her to your shoulder again.

If your baby continues to swallow air, feed him in a more upright position, which allows gravity to hold the heavier milk down and let the lighter air rise to the top of his stomach where it can be burped out more easily. Also burp your baby in an upright position. Place a "bubble cloth" over your shoulder and hold your baby against it, firmly patting and stroking his back, or walk around and rock him rhythmically. Avoid jostling your baby too much, which may aggravate the colic.

Develop your own individual "colic" carry. Parents who have survived and comforted their colicky babies have learned what position works most of the time to ease the colic. Massaging your baby's abdomen also can help move the gas through her intestines so it can pass out the rectum. Start by warming her tummy with a warm washcloth or warm heating pad (be careful not to overdo this heat on very tender skin). Then use your flattened hand to stroke in the direction of the large intestine, up, over, and down. As you do this, you may feel a pocket of gas. Your baby must be relaxed for this to be very effective.

One way to get a screaming, rigid baby to stop crying and relax long enough to eliminate his gas is a bit unusual, but it may be just the thing that works for you. Tape record your baby's cry (about two minutes' worth) and play it back, being sure he can hear it above his uproar. When he hears it, he will stop to listen and may relax long enough to be massaged or to pass some gas on his own.

Milk allergy may be the cause of your infant's colic, even if you are breastfeeding. You may have an allergen in your milk because of the cow's milk in your diet. Temporarily remove dairy products from your diet to see if this makes a difference in your infant's colic. If you choose to remain off dairy products, consult your doctor to be sure you are getting the proper substitute nutrition. If you are formula-feeding, change to a less allergenic formula and seek advice from your physician.

Gastroesophageal reflux, the regurgitation of stomach acids into the esophagus, may irritate the esophagus causing a heartburn-like pain and therefore irritability in the baby being labeled colicky. If your baby wakes in pain at night, then suspect a medical cause such as reflux. Ordinary colic usually does not affect a baby consistently during sleep. If you suspect this condition, consult your doctor. Spitting up does not always occur with reflux, so the diagnosis may require testing.

What appears to be colic in some babies actually may be their temperaments, and their fussiness results in a total family problem. These babies are more appropriately termed *high-need babies*. See Chapter 4 for an in-depth discussion of the high-need baby. Many of the survival tips listed for parenting a high-need child are also appropriate for the colicky baby.

There is an old saying in pediatrics concerning many of the problems of young childhood: "It soon will pass." This is very true of colic. Most babies' colic disappears when they are between three and six months old. By that time, they are sitting upright and their intestines are more mature. Their parents have learned to cope with the colic and to gentle their fussy babies, and the babies have achieved a better feeling of rightness. If your baby has persistent colic, don't forget to pray to God, asking Him to relieve the pain in His little child.

Cow's Milk Allergy

Cow's milk allergy is one of the most commonly overlooked causes of illness in young infants. Because of the high incidence of milk allergy in babies younger than a year and because drinking large volumes of cow's milk may cause anemia, the American Academy of Pediatrics recommends that infants not be given cow's milk before they are one year old.

Why is cow's milk so allergenic? The protein in cow's milk is suited for the intestines of a cow. Exposing human intestines to this protein may cause the gastrointestinal tract to bleed in small amounts, which results in anemia, vomiting, diarrhea, abdominal pain, lower intestinal gas, and bloating. These allergenic proteins also may be absorbed into your child's bloodstream, causing the systemic symptoms of allergies: an eczema-like rash, runny nose, or wheezing. Also, repeated colds and ear infections may be caused or aggravated by milk allergies.

Sometimes the intestines of older children cannot

digest the sugar (lactose) in cow's milk. This results in a condition called "lactose intolerance" in which undigested lactose accumulates in the large intestines and forms gas, causing a bloated feeling, abdominal pain, and diarrhea. Because many mammals become lactose intolerant after they are weaned, it is possible that lactose intolerance is a normal process of maturity and that some children who are weaned from human milk to cow's milk really do outgrow their need for milk.

If your child is allergic to cow's milk, breastfeed him as long as you can. The longer your infant is breastfed, the less likely he is to develop a cow's milk allergy in later childhood. If your family has a long history of allergies, I strongly advise you to withhold dairy products for at least one to two years.

There is no good nutritional reason for discontinuing formula as long as your infant likes it. Consult your doctor before deciding to use a less allergenic formula that is not based on cow's milk. Allergic reactions to cow's milk protein usually disappear by two to three years of age in most children. The lactose intolerance may, however, persist throughout childhood and even adulthood.

A child who will not drink her milk may in fact be allergic to milk. If you suspect your child is allergic to milk, withhold milk and dairy products from her diet for at least three to four weeks to see if her symptoms disappear. Then challenge her again with milk to see if the symptoms reappear. Repeat the process. If your child has improved on the milk-free diet in two successive trials, then she probably is allergic to cow's milk.

If your child cannot tolerate milk, you do not need to worry that she will not get enough calcium. There is some calcium in most foods, especially whole grains and vegetables. Since dairy products are still the prime source of calcium for most children, try feeding your child yogurts and some cheeses because the allergens often are changed in the processing. Like formula, yogurt has all the nutritional benefits of milk without the problems of lactose intolerance. Yogurt is made by adding a bacterial culture to milk; the culture ferments the milk and breaks down the lactose into simple sugars which are absorbed more easily.

Food Allergy

Food allergies ("food intolerance" may be more medically correct) often are called the "great masqueraders" because they mask a variety of symptoms in children that often go undetected. The most common symptoms of food allergies are eczema-like rashes (especially on the face), puffy eyelids, chronic diarrhea, and a persistently stuffy nose. Sometimes the symptoms of food allergies may be very subtle: a pale, tired, or droopy child; a child with headaches, abdominal pain, or muscle aches; or a child with recurrent colds and ear infections; night waking may be the only symptom in some children.

The most common food allergens in order of their prevalence are milk and dairy products, chocolate, eggs, cane sugar, citrus fruits, nuts, wheat products, corn, berries, and food colorings and additives. If you suspect your child is allergic to any of these foods, you may have to do a bit of detective work. Eliminate the suspected food allergens one by one from your child's diet until the most obvious symptoms disappear. Then include them in his diet a second time to see if the symptoms reappear. If you strongly suspect your child has a food allergy, consult your doctor for a proper way to use an elimination diet. If you have a strong family history of allergies, the following suggestions may help you prevent allergies in your child: (1) breastfeed your infant for at least one year; (2) delay introducing solid foods until your infant shows definite signs of wanting solid foods; (3) begin with the less allergenic foods (rice, bananas, yellow vegetables); (4) avoid giving a mixture of food to your infant who is less than one year old because if he is allergic to the mixture, isolating the offending allergen will be difficult; and (5) withhold potentially allergenic foods (see the previous list) until your child is more than one year old.

Junk Food

Two types of food rightfully earn the title "junk food": foods that have artificial food colorings (mainly, red and yellow dyes) and cane sugar. This "table sugar" is processed so heavily that the few nutrients found in natural sugar are removed. This refined sugar is absorbed more rapidly from the intestines than other kinds of sugar and reaches a high concentration in the blood. This triggers the release of insulin which rapidly lowers the blood sugar, causing behavioral changes and often stimulating the person to eat again.

The child's developing brain is very dependent on a steady blood sugar as its prime source of energy. Fluctuations in his blood sugar can cause hyperactivity, fainting, irritability, depression, and aggression. Children with marked blood-sugar swings frequently have difficulty concentrating, and their learning is often compromised. Headaches, visual disturbances, and a general tired feeling are symptoms also associated with low blood sugar.

Not all sugar should be considered junk food since our bodies derive about 45 percent of their necessary calories from sugars, including the sugars that occur in the form of starches (grains and vegetables). The refined cane sugar or corn syrup, also called "dextrose" on some labels, is what I mean by "junk sugar." Nutritious sugars are the natural sugars such as the lactose in milk and the fructose in fruits. These sugars are absorbed and utilized within the body differently from how junk sugar is used. They cause fewer swings in blood sugar and, therefore, do not adversely affect a child's behavior. These sugars also contain small amounts of additional nutrients, such as vitamins and traces of minerals.

How can you know whether or not the sugar added to foods is junk sugar? Current label laws require contents to be listed in order of volume. If sugar is high on the list of contents, the food is very high in sugar. If the label says "corn syrup," "sugar," or "dextrose," the food is high in junk sugars. Natural sugars will be listed as honey or fructose.

Highly colored and highly sugared fruit drinks, soft drinks, and punches rank high among junk foods. Besides containing food colorings (which also may trigger behavior problems in some children) and junk sugar, these drinks contain very little, if any, actual juice, have limited nutritional value, and definitely should not be given to children.

Feeding your baby often dominates your thinking during his or her first year of life. Also consuming great energy and sometimes worry is the prevention and overcoming of common childhood illnesses.

CHAPTER 7

COMMON MEDICAL CONCERNS OF BABY'S FIRST YEAR

■ The most effective health care system set up in most locations throughout North America is the system of well-baby care. In this system your child is examined by your physician at periodic intervals, usually birth; two weeks; two, four, six, nine, twelve, fifteen, eighteen, and twenty-four months; two-and-a-half and three years; and once a year thereafter.

This schedule may vary according to the parents' needs and the baby's general health. The purposes of these periodic exams are (1) to check for actual or potential abnormalities in growth and development; (2) to note your child's nutritional requirements at various ages; (3) to discuss developmental and emotional changes; (4) to point out specific age- and stage-related needs; (5) to discuss your questions or adjustment problems; (6) to help your doctor get to know you and your child during the child's well state, which serves as a reference point for medical judgment when your child is ill; (7) to treat the illnesses or abnormalities that may be detected during examination even though your child appears well; and (8) to administer necessary immunizations.

Just as parents are developing intuition about their child in the early stages of parenting, the pediatrician also is developing an intuition about your child and about you as parents. It is very important for your doctor to know your child. Nothing is more frustrating for a doctor than to see the child only when he is ill. The doctor will feel he or she does not know the total child and is therefore at a disadvantage when it is necessary to make appropriate medical decisions. Scheduling periodic exams is the best preventive medicine, and it is also an economically wise investment in the long run.

Getting the most out of your visits to your doctor can be summed up by one word, *communication*. Shortly before your appointment, make a list of your concerns. Memorize this list, because I have found that new parents often forget to bring their lists. Being well prepared when you visit your doctor conveys that these visits are important to you and your child. If possible, both parents should attend these well-child visits since this also conveys the message of commitment.

Another kind of doctor's visit is for a specific problem. Because illnesses cannot be conveniently scheduled, your doctor will usually reserve some time during each office day for treating sudden illnesses. Please limit your discussion to the specific problem for which you brought your child to the office, since your doctor is probably fitting your child in between patients already scheduled.

A behavior or psychological problem may require a visit to the doctor. Since these visits usually require more time, request a long appointment and indicate to the receptionist the purpose of your appointment.

Common Medical Concerns

Sniffles

Sometime in his first few weeks you may think your baby has his first cold. These noisy, gurgling sounds are usually not colds (meaning an infection), but they certainly may sound like a cold and be a source of great concern. Babies do not breathe the ways adults do. Adults are able to breathe through their noses or their mouths, and their air passages are relatively large. Babies are predominantly nose breathers, and their air passages are relatively small. For these reasons, even a slight amount of congestion in the nose or throat may bother them. Sniffles in tiny babies are caused more by environmental irritants than by infections. The most common irritants are lint from blankets and clothing, dust, chemical fumes, and cigarette smoke. In fact, children of smoking parents do have more colds than children of nonsmoking parents.

Another cause of clogged nasal passages is very dry air, especially in the winter months that require central heating. As a general guide, when the heat goes on, so should a humidifier. A tiny baby cannot blow his own nose. You must do it for him, and the following suggestions will help you accomplish this.

Clearing your baby's nose. Squirt a few drops of saline nose drops (available without prescription at the pharmacy) into each nostril. The drops often loosen the secretions and stimulate your baby to sneeze them toward the front part of his nose. Next, take a rubber-bulb syringe, called a "nasal aspirator," or a rubber ear syringe and gently suck out the loosened secretions.

When to clear your baby's nose. Signs of a baby's obstructed nasal passages include frequent waking up, inability to sustain nursing (he needs his mouth to breathe), and breathing with his mouth open. If your baby sleeps comfortably with his mouth closed and he has not changed his nursing pattern, you do not need to clean out his nose even though he may sound noisy.

Sometime around his first or second month, your baby may experience what is called the "two-month cold." Again, this is probably not a cold. Babies often make more saliva than they are able to handle initially. As a result, the saliva collects in the back of their throats, causing noisy, gurgly breathing. You also may hear and feel a "rattle" in his chest, but the problem is not really in his chest. What you hear and feel is the air moving past the vibrating mucous in the back of his throat, producing sounds and vibrations like a musical instrument. These secretions are often too far back to get with a nasal aspirator, and the baby's problem is usually not in his nose anyway. Keeping a vaporizer running while he is sleeping often will thin these secretions. These throaty noises occur less when your baby is sleeping since saliva production usually lessens with sleep. These noises may continue during the first six months and may become more noticeable during times of teething. As soon as your baby begins to spend more of his time in an upright position and learns how to swallow the excess saliva, these noises gradually disappear. (See the section on colds later in this chapter for ways to recognize and treat actual infection.)

Eye Discharges

In a baby's first few months, discharging eyes are usually caused by blocked tear ducts. Most infants begin tearing by three weeks of age, and these tears should drain from the nasal corners of the eyes through the tear ducts. At birth, the nasal ends of these ducts are closed by a thin membrane that usually breaks open shortly after birth allowing the proper drainage of the tears. Often this membrane does not open fully, the tear ducts remain plugged, and tears accumulate in one or both eyes. There is a general principle of the human body that if fluid does not drain properly, it soon will become infected. As a result, the discharge from your baby's eyes may become persistently yellow, indicating that these tears have become infected in the region of the blocked tear ducts.

Treating blocked tear ducts. Gently massage the tear duct which is located beneath the tiny "bump" in the nasal corner of each eye. Massage in an upward direction (toward the eye) about six times. Do this as frequently as you think of it during the day, for example, before each diaper change. If you properly massage the tear duct, this pressure on the fluid trapped within the ducts should pop open the membrane and clear the tear ducts. If you notice persistent tearing or yellow discharge from one or both eyes, mention this to your doctor during your baby's checkup, and your doctor will instruct you in the proper treatment of this condition. Blocked tear ducts usually clear up by six months of age. Occasionally, it is necessary for an eye doctor to open these ducts by inserting a tiny probe into them, but this should not be done until a satisfactory trial of massage and eye drops has been attempted.

Thrush

Thrush is a common yeast infection in the baby's mouth that looks like white cottage-cheese patches on the inner cheeks, inner lips, tongue, and roof of the mouth. This fungus infection seldom bothers the baby, and it is easily treated by a prescription that is painted on the white patches. The baby also may have a similar diaper rash which may need prescription medication. Sometimes the baby may transfer the infection to the mother's nipples during nursing, causing some tenderness, so that a prescription cream may be necessary to treat her too.

Common Skin Rashes

Normal baby "marks." Most newborn babies have smooth, reddish pink marks on the back of the neck, on the forehead, between the eyes, and on the upper eyelids. These are not really rashes but are areas of skin where the blood vessels are prominent and show through the baby's thin skin. These areas often become more noticeable when the baby cries. As your baby grows and accumulates more fat beneath her skin, her reddish areas become less noticeable and probably will disappear by one year of age.

Birthmarks. The most common kind of birthmark looks like a small strawberry and is called a "hemangioma." It is caused by the proliferation of tiny blood vessels within the skin. It may not be present at birth but may appear within a baby's first few months. Hemangiomas gradually grow larger, begin to dry up by turning a grayish color in the center, and usually disappear within several years. Five percent of these hemangiomas are "rapid growing" and need to be watched carefully—they may require laser surgery.

Non-Caucasian babies often have bluish birthmarks on the skin of the lower back which look like bruises. These normal spots usually disappear with time but may remain until adulthood.

Milia are tiny, whitish, pin-head-sized bumps most prominent on the face, especially on the skin of the nose. This rash is caused by oily secretions plugging the pores of the skin, but it disappears after gently washing with warm water and mild soap.

Newborn "acne." Newborns often have a pimply, oily rash on the face resembling acne, which appears several weeks after birth. The increased hormone levels at birth cause the oil glands of the face to swell. The acne-like rash can be removed easily with gentle washings with warm water and a mild soap.

Seborrhea is a crusty, oily rash that appears behind the ears and on the scalp. In addition to washing with warm water, a prescription cream may be needed.

Cradle cap is a crusty, oily, plaquelike rash on the baby's scalp, most common over the soft spot. Cradle cap is best treated by massaging vegetable oil into the crusty areas and gently removing the softened scales with a washcloth or soft, fine-toothed comb. If this rash persists, a special shampoo and a prescription cream may be needed.

The skin, especially that of a newborn baby, enjoys high humidity. This is why most of these rashes seem to be worse during the winter when central heating dries the air. A humidifier in the baby's sleeping room often will lessen these rashes.

Prickly heat rashes are tiny pimples with red bases and clear centers. Prickly heat usually appears in areas of the skin where there is excessive moisture retention, such as behind the ears, between the neck folds, in the groin, and in areas where clothing fits tightly. This rash is treated by gently washing the area in plain, cold water or with a solution of baking soda (one teaspoon to a cup of water). Dressing your baby in lightweight, loose-fitting clothing also should soothe his rash.

Diaper rash. Human skin, especially the sensitive skin of a newborn baby, was not designed to be in prolonged contact with wet cloth. Diaper rashes are caused by the chemical irritation of the ammonia formed by the urine and the mechanical rubbing of moist cloth on sensitive skin. The following suggestions are for the prevention and treatment of your baby's diaper rash.

1. Experiment with both cloth diapers and disposable diapers to see which one causes fewer rashes. If you use disposable diapers be sure to fold the edge of the diaper down so the plastic lining does not touch your baby's skin.

2. Change wet diapers as quickly as possible. If diaper rash is a persistent problem, change your baby when he wakes during the night also, or use double or triple cloth diapers.

3. After each diaper change, wash your baby's diaper area with plain water or mild soap, rinse well, and gently blot dry. Avoid strong soaps and excessive rubbing on already sensitive skin. A very red but not raised rash is often caused by an "acid burn" due to the acidic nature of your baby's stools (usually following a treatment with antibiotics).

4. Soak your baby's bottom in a baking soda bath (a tablespoon of baking soda in two quarts of water

in his tub). After soaking the baby's bottom, give a "sniff test" to detect any smell of ammonia.

5. Allow the diaper area to "breathe." Avoid tight-fitting diapers and rubber pants, which retain moisture. Reserve rubber pants for occasions where being a baby may not be socially acceptable. Place rubber pads underneath your baby to protect his bedding. Expose your baby's diaper area as much as possible to the air. While he is sleeping, unfold the diaper and lay it beneath him. In warm weather, let your baby nap outside with his bare bottom exposed to fresh air.

6. Creams and pastes are usually not necessary when your baby's skin is not irritated. Attempt to treat the diaper rash early before the skin breaks down and becomes infected. At the first sign of a reddened, irritated bottom, apply a barrier cream such as zinc oxide. Barrier creams also should be used during times when your baby has diarrhea, such as when he is teething or has an intestinal infection. Avoid cornstarch on the diaper area because it encourages growth of fungi.

7. Fungus diaper rashes are red, raised, rough, sore-looking rashes that have tiny pustules and are resistant to simple forms of treatment. This yeast-infection kind of diaper rash is treated by a prescription cream and the measures noted here.

Fever

What constitutes a fever? A rectal temperature greater than 100.5 degrees Fahrenheit (38 degrees Celsius) may be considered a fever. Most children have a normal oral body temperature of 98.6 degrees Fahrenheit (37 degrees Celsius), but normal temperature varies among children from 97 to 100 degrees Fahrenheit (37 to 38 degrees Celsius). Many children show normal daily fluctuations in body temperature. It may be lower in the morning and during rest and a degree higher in the late afternoon or during strenuous exercise.

What causes fever? Fever is a symptom of an underlying illness, but it is not an illness itself. Normal body temperature is maintained by a thermostat in a tiny organ of the brain called the "hypothalamus," which regulates the balance between the heat produced and the heat lost in the body. A fever occurs when more heat is produced in the body than can be released, thus raising your child's temperature. Germs from infection within your child's body release substances into the blood stream called "pyrogens" (heat-producing substances), which cause a fever. Any time there is a change from normal body temperature, the thermostat reacts to bring that temperature back to normal; for example, when your child is cold, he shivers to produce heat. When your child is warm or has a fever, the blood vessels of his skin become larger (as evidenced by his flushed cheeks), and his heart beats faster. These mechanisms cause more blood to reach the surface of the skin and release the excess body heat. A child with fever also sweats to cool his body by evaporation and breathes faster to get rid of the warm air. In addition to having these general signs of fever, a child may have headaches, muscle aches, and general fatigue.

How to take your child's temperature. You may take your child's temperature in three places: the rectum (rectally), the armpit (axillarily), and the mouth (orally). Rectal temperature is one-half to one degree higher than oral temperature, and axillary temperature is usually one degree lower than oral.

Rectal thermometers are easiest and safest to use on children less than five years old. Follow these steps to take your child's rectal temperature.

1. Use a rectal thermometer (one with a rounded, stubby end that is marked "rectal").
2. Shake down the thermometer with a wrist-snapping motion until the mercury column is below 95 degrees Fahrenheit.
3. Grease the bulb end with petroleum jelly.
4. Lay your child facedown across your lap.
5. Gently insert the thermometer bulb about one inch into the rectum allowing the thermometer to seek its own path. Don't force it.
6. Hold the thermometer between your index and middle fingers (like a cigarette) with the palm of your hand and your fingers grasping your child's buttocks. By holding your child in this position you can hold the thermometer and keep your child from moving. Never leave a child alone with the thermometer in place.
7. Try to keep the thermometer in place for three minutes. The rectal reading will be within a degree of the true temperature after one minute.
8. Practice "feeling" your child's temperature by placing the palm of your hand on her forehead or by kissing her forehead so that you are used to telling when she has a fever. Then confirm it by taking her temperature with a thermometer.
9. Keep a temperature chart by writing down the time, your child's temperature, and the methods you have used to treat the fever.
10. The new ear thermometers are easier on parents and children, and although they are not as precise

as rectal thermometers, they are accurate enough and reliable as long as they are used according to the manufacturer's specifications.

A child more than five years of age will usually cooperate with having his temperature taken orally. Follow these three steps.

1. Use an oral thermometer (the oral thermometer has a longer, thinner shaft than the rectal thermometer and is marked "oral"). Shake down the thermometer as described in the paragraph on rectal thermometers.
2. Have your child lie or sit quietly and place the mercury end of the thermometer under his tongue, slightly to one side. Instruct him to keep his mouth closed and close his lips firmly but not hold the thermometer in his teeth. Allowing the child to open his mouth to breathe with the thermometer in place may make the temperature reading inaccurate.
3. Try to keep the thermometer in place with the mouth closed for two to three minutes.

If your child resists having his temperature taken orally, you might try to take an axillary reading. An oral thermometer may be used for an axillary temperature, but three to four minutes is required to achieve a stable temperature reading.

When to worry about fever. Two kinds of infections cause fever: viral and bacterial. Viral infections are usually less worrisome and show the following features: (1) the fever comes on suddenly in a previously well child; (2) the fever is usually very high (103 to 105 degrees Fahrenheit); (3) the fever is easily brought down by the methods mentioned in the section on how to treat your child's fever; and (4) the child seems to feel better when the fever is brought down. When their children have viral infections, parents often say, "I am surprised the fever is so high because my child does not look or act that sick." The most common viral infection in the first year of life is called "roseola," which produces a very high fever (103 to 105 degrees Fahrenheit) for about three days, but there are no other symptoms and the child does not appear as ill as the high fever would indicate. After the fever breaks, a faint, generalized, reddish pink rash appears and lasts for less than twenty-four hours.

In a bacterial infection the temperature may not be as high as that of a viral infection, but the fever does not come down as easily with the methods recommended for treating your child's fever. Also when your child has a bacterial infection, he acts as sick as his high fever would indicate.

When to call your doctor about fever. Remember, your doctor is interested in how sick your child looks and acts rather than how high the temperature is. If your child does not act particularly sick, administer all the recommended methods to lower your child's temperature before calling your doctor. How your child responds to temperature-lowering methods is one of the main concerns your doctor will ask you about. The younger the infant, the more worrisome the fever. Any fever in an infant less than four months old should be reported immediately to your doctor. If your child's temperature cannot be lowered by using the methods suggested in the next section, and if he is rapidly becoming more ill, call your doctor. Also call your doctor if obvious signs and symptoms associated with a fever, such as ear pain, severe cough, sore throat, any problems associated with urination appear. These symptoms may indicate a bacterial infection.

When examining your feverish child, your doctor is attempting to determine whether the fever is caused by a virus or a bacteria. Bacterial infections need antibiotics; viral infections usually do not but may be treated by the methods indicated in the following section. Sometimes it is difficult to determine the kind of infection, and your doctor may perform some laboratory tests to help make this decision. Or your doctor may elect to wait a day or so before making a definite decision and request that you notify him of your child's progress.

Because of the common difficulty of determining the kind of infection, it is very important for you to report to your doctor if your child's general condition worsens; your doctor may have to revise his diagnosis. Viral infections usually last three to five days and gradually subside. Bacterial infections, however, usually worsen if untreated.

How to treat your child's fever. You can lower your child's temperature with two basic mechanisms: (1) giving your child medications, such as aspirin, acetaminophen, or ibuprofen, which reset her thermostat, and (2) using methods to get rid of excess body heat as described in this section. It is necessary to lower your child's thermostat with medications before using heat removal procedures. Your child's thermostat is set so that if her body temperature is lowered, her body is programmed to produce more heat and therefore raise her body temperature again. For example, removing a child's clothing and placing her in a bath with water cooler than her body temperature will signal her thermostat and cause her to shiver to produce heat and her blood vessels to constrict in order to conserve heat. The medications will reset the thermostat so that when the child's temperature is lowered by cooling, her body will not react to produce more heat. An example of this mechanism is evident in the way heat is regulated in your house. If your house is too warm, you lower the thermostat and then open the windows. If you open the windows first without resetting the thermostat, heat production continues and your house remains warm.

The most commonly used medications to lower a temperature nowadays are non-aspirin acetaminophen or ibuprofen. *Acetaminophen* (Tylenol, Tempra, Liquiprin, or Panadol) and *ibuprofen* (Advil or Motrin) are medications that (1) lower your child's fever, and (2) help relieve some of the general aches and pains that often accompany childhood illnesses. They are generally recommended instead of aspirin for the young child for the following reasons: (1) they are not linked with Reye's Syndrome (explained in the aspirin section on the following pages); (2) they are also available in liquid form and therefore easier to administer than tablets to the young child; and (3) they do not keep building up in your child's blood with prolonged usage and are less likely to produce an overdose with routine use as is the case with aspirin.

Acetaminophen is available in the following forms: (1) drops: 0.8 milliliters equals 80 milligrams; (2) elixir: 5 milliliters (one teaspoon equals 160 milligrams); (3) tablets (chewable): one tablet equals 80 milligrams; and (4) adult tablets (regular strength): one tablet equals 325 milligrams. Ibuprofen is available in the following forms: (1) drops: 1.25 milliliters equals 50 milligrams; (2) liquid: 5 milliliters (one teaspoon equals 100 milligrams); (3) tablets (chewable): one tablet equals 100 milligrams; and (4) adult tablets: one tablet equals 200 milligrams.

The following dosage schedules for acetaminophen and ibuprofen will help you determine the proper dosage for your child.

Acetaminophen (Tylenol)

Age Group	0–3 mos.	4–11 mos.	12–23 mos.	2–3 yrs.
Weight (lbs.)	6–11	12–17	18–23	24–35
Dose of Tylenol in milligrams	40	80	120	160
Drops (80 mg/0.8 ml)	½	1	1½	2
Elixir (160 mg/5 ml)	—	½	¾	1
Chewable tablets (80 mg each)	—	—	1½	2

Age Group	4–5 yrs.	6–8 yrs.	9–10 yrs.	11–12 yrs.
Weight (lbs.)	36–47	48–59	60–71	72–95
Dose of Tylenol in milligrams	240	320	400	480
Drops (80 mg/0.8 ml)	3	4	5	—
Elixir (160 mg/5 ml)	1½	2	2½	3
Chewable tablets (80 mg each)	3	4	5	6

Doses should be administered 4 or 5 times daily—but not to exceed 5 doses in 24 hours. (The above recommendations are for Tylenol. The dosage schedule for other brands of acetaminophen may vary.)

Ibuprofen (Motrin)

Age Group	0–3 mos.	4–11 mos.	12–23 mos.	2–3 yrs.
Weight (lbs.)	6–11	12–17	18–23	24–35
Dose of Motrin in milligrams	25	50	75	100
Drops (50 mg/1.25 ml)	½	1	1½	2
Liquid (100 mg/5 ml)	–	½	¾	1
Chewable tablets (100 mg each)	–	–	1½	2

Age Group	4–5 yrs.	6–8 yrs.	9–10 yrs.	11–12 yrs.
Weight (lbs.)	36–47	48–59	60–71	72–95
Dose of Motrin in milligrams	150	200	250	300
Drops (50 mg/1.25 ml)	3	4	5	–
Liquid (100 mg/5 ml)	1½	2	2½	3
Chewable tablets (100 mg each)	3	4	5	6

Doses should be administered 4 or 5 times daily—but not to exceed 5 doses in 24 hours. (The above recommendations are for Motrin. The dosage schedule for other brands of ibuprofen may vary.)

Aspirin is still used as a fever reducer and pain reliever, but usually under a doctor's recommendation and supervision. With aspirin, if the dosage is too high, your child may become ill from aspirin overdose. The following dosage schedule is based on the most up-to-date research and is designed to be both safe and effective.

Aspirin Dosage by Age

Age in years	1	2	3	4	5	6	7	8	9	10	11	12
No. of 1¼ gr. tablets given every 4–6 hours	1	2	2	3	3	4	4	4	5	5	6	8 *or 2 adult aspirin*

This dosage schedule is based upon giving your child aspirin every four hours around the clock. Since it is usually unwise to wake a sleeping child who has a fever, most children miss one or two doses each day, thus making the schedule slightly conservative. Children's aspirin, or baby aspirin, comes in one and one-quarter grain tablets (seventy-five milligrams). The dosage schedule is based on a child's age and is a rough guide for selecting a safe and effective aspirin dosage. If you wish to be precise, you may calculate your child's dosage by this method: five milligrams of aspirin per pound of body weight (ten milligrams of aspirin per kilogram of body weight) given every four hours. One adult aspirin, which is five grains, is equivalent to four children's aspirin.

Aspirin overdose. In order to avoid an overdose of aspirin, if you have given your child the appropriate dosage around the clock for forty-eight hours, check with your physician before administering any more. Current packaging laws have greatly reduced accidental aspirin poisoning in children. Even if a child younger than five years old ingested a whole bottle of children's aspirin, aspirin poisoning would be unlikely. As a rough guide, if your child does not take more than one baby aspirin per pound of body weight, he is unlikely to suffer any ill effects. If your child ingests any higher dosage than this, certainly call your doctor or your local poison control center. Adult aspirin preparations pose a greater chance of accidental poisoning than children's tablets, which means that you should take greater precaution with your bottles of aspirin than with your children's aspirin. If you child does take more than a safe amount of aspirin, call your doctor or local poison control center for instructions. When administering aspirin, it is usually best to give your child an increased amount of fluids to help wash the aspirin through his system.

Generally, aspirin is a safe and effective fever-lowering medication for most children. When used during certain viral illnesses such as chicken pox or the flu, aspirin has been incriminated as a possible cause of a serious brain and liver disease called "Reye's Syndrome." The cause-effect relationship of aspirin and Reye's Syndrome is still not proven, but at this writing it is recommended that aspirin *not* be used for these conditions.

Other ways to lower your child's fever. In addition to using aspirin or acetaminophen to reset your child's thermostat, the following methods will help remove the excess heat from your child's system.

1. *Undress your child completely,* or at most, dress him in light, loose-fitting clothing. This allows the excess heat to radiate out of his body into the cooler environment. Avoid the tendency to bundle up your child when he has a fever because this will only cause his body to retain heat.

2. *Keep your child's environment cold.* Decrease the temperature in his room, open a window slightly, use an air conditioner or a nearby fan. A "draft" will not bother your child. This cool air helps remove the heat that is radiating out of his body. Yes, your child may go outside when he has a fever. The fresh, circulating air is good for him.

3. *Give your child a lot of extra fluids* when he has a fever because excess body heat causes him to lose fluids. Give him cool, clear liquids in small, frequent amounts.

4. *Give your child a cooling bath.* If in spite of all these other measures your child's temperature remains over 103 degrees Fahrenheit (39.5 degrees Celsius), or if she continues to be uncomfortable with the fever, place her in a tub of water and run the water all the way up to her neck. The water temperature should be warm enough not to be uncomfortable but cooler than her body temperature. If the young child protests this tub bath and begins to cry, sit in the bathtub with her and amuse her with her favorite floating toys. Crying and struggling will only increase her temperature. Keeping your child in the cooling bath for twenty to thirty minutes should bring her temperature down a couple of degrees. During the bath, rub her with a washcloth to stimulate more circulation to the skin and increase heat loss. After the bath, gently pat your child dry, leaving a slight excess of water on her skin, which will

evaporate and produce a further cooling effect. Do not use alcohol rubs because they may produce shivering and toxic vapors. If your child's temperature zooms back up again, it may be necessary to repeat the tub bath.

Can fever be dangerous? In most children, the fever itself is not dangerous. Fever does make children very uncomfortable, creating a general feeling of muscle aches and pains. The main reason for controlling high temperatures in young children is the danger of febrile convulsions. The young child's brain does not tolerate sudden temperature fluctuations and may react with a convulsion. It is not so much how high the fever is but how fast the temperature rises that causes convulsions. Most febrile convulsions can be prevented by using all the methods to control temperature just described. Febrile convulsions, while alarming to parents, seldom harm the child. The frequency and severity of these convulsions lessen as your child gets older and seldom occur in a child more than five years old.

Because a child with a fever is often uncomfortable, keep his body quiet and his soul at peace. Pray for your child, asking God to relieve his fever and the illness producing his discomfort.

Colds

What is a cold? In medical terms, colds are called "upper respiratory infections" (URI), which means an infection of the lining of the air passages: nose, sinuses, throat, ears, and larynx. Germs, either viruses or bacteria, infect the lining of these air passages, and the tissue of this lining reacts by swelling and secreting mucous. The runny nose and the child's postnasal drip are caused by the accumulation of mucous. Your child may

133

then sneeze and cough, which are his body's defense mechanisms, to clear this mucous. Swelling of the tissues accounts for many of the signs of colds: swelling of the nasal membranes causes a child to breathe noisily through his mouth; swelling of the veins and tissues beneath the eyelids causes a bluish discoloration; swelling of the tonsils and adenoids causes the throaty noises most commonly heard at night; swelling of the larynx causes the croupy, seal-bark cough. Most children have several colds per year. The school-age child is a very social being and "shares" her cold germs with other children. As the child grows, her immunity to various germs increases, and the number and severity of colds gradually decrease.

Although colds are, strictly speaking, caused by infections, allergies may also account for swelling and mucous secretion. The germs may settle in these secretions resulting in an infection. It is common for young children to have both allergy colds and infection colds.

When is a cold more than a cold? The "common cold," as it is often called, is usually caused by a virus and subsides with the general measures mentioned here. However, it is important for parents to recognize when a cold needs a consultation with the doctor. The following general guidelines will help you decide when to take your child to a doctor for a cold.

Determine how much the cold is bothering your child. If your child is happy and playful, eats well, sleeps well, and is not particularly bothered by the cold, then it is mostly likely a viral infection. This cold is simply a noisy nuisance and probably will subside with proper treatment.

Check the mucous coming from his nose. If the secretions are clear and watery and your child is generally happy, his cold is most likely caused by a virus. If the discharge from his nose becomes thick and yellow or green and persists that way throughout the day, and if your child becomes increasingly cranky and awakens more at night, he probably has a bacterial infection. Medical advice should be obtained. The eyes are often the mirror of the cold's severity. If your child has a persistently yellow drainage from his eyes, most likely he has an underlying sinus or ear infection and should be examined by your doctor. In my office we follow "Dr. Bill's rule": if your child's nose progresses from runny to snotty and his behavior progresses from happy to cranky, your child should be examined by a doctor.

When is a cold contagious? If your child has a fever, snotty nose, and cough, consider him contagious and keep him out of the church nursery. Children are most contagious the first few days of the cold. It is not necessary to quarantine a child who has no fever, is not sick, and has only a clear running nose or slight cough.

How should you treat a cold? General treatment of the simple cold is aimed at keeping the nasal discharge thin and moving. Secretions that become stagnant are likely to result in a worsening infection. Use a vaporizer while your child is sleeping. Do not add anything to the water in the vaporizer since an additive could irritate your child's respiratory passages. Give your child a lot of fluids to drink. Clear the nasal passages. Encourage the older child to blow her nose well and not to sniff the secretions back up into her sinuses.

Over-the-counter medications for colds are called "decongestants." They are designed to dry up the secretions and shrink the swelling of the lining of the respiratory passages. In my experience, these medications have had limited usefulness for children. If a child is given a high enough dosage of a decongestant to help the cold, he may experience the undesirable side effects of drowsiness or hyperexcitability, rapid heartbeat, or nightmares. Dosages recommended on the package inserts are often so low as to be ineffective.

Decongestants are more effective for colds produced by allergies than for those produced by infections. Overuse of decongestants may, in fact, dry up the secretions to the extent that the child cannot cough up the secretions. Thus the cold worsens. Nose drops for a persistently runny nose that is really bothering the child may be effective, but they should not be used more than twice a day or for more than three days at a time. Most of these over-the-counter remedies are used in desperation to give the child some relief. It is best to check with your doctor before using any over-the-counter medication.

Antibiotics for colds. Viral infections generally do not need antibiotics, but bacterial infections do. This is the judgment your doctor tries to make when examining your child for a cold. Your doctor listens to your child's chest and looks into his nose, throat, and ears to determine if there are any signs of bacterial infection. If there are not, your doctor may say to you, "This is a viral infection, which does not need an antibiotic, and your child should get better by simply giving him fluids and cleaning out his nose. But call me if he gets worse." Keep in mind that you are going to your doctor primarily for consultation, not necessarily for medication. Do not be disappointed if your doctor "doesn't find anything." It often requires more judgment *not* to treat an illness with antibiotics than to treat one with them. Remember your doctor's closing statement to call if your child gets worse, since viral infections may progress to bacterial infections and a change of treatment may be necessary. If your doctor suspects your child's cold is caused by a bacterial infection, an appropriate antibiotic may be prescribed. Be sure to complete the entire course of the prescribed antibiotic, otherwise the partially treated infection may recur.

Ear Infections

Because of the frequency and severity of ear infections in young children, you should have a full understanding of their causes and treatment. Children harbor germs in the secretions of the nose and throat to which they have not yet become immune. Because of the proximity of the nose and throat to the ears, germs commonly travel up the eustachian tube into the ear during a cold.

The eustachian tube in children often functions inadequately. The eustachian tube has two main functions: (1) to equalize the air pressure on both sides of the eardrum, which allows the eardrum to vibrate freely, and produce sound, and (2) to drain the middle ear of fluid and germs that may collect during a cold. A child's eustachian tube is short, wide, straight, and at a horizontal angle, all of which allows germs to travel more easily from the throat up into the middle ear. As your child grows, the eustachian tube becomes longer, narrower, and at a more acute angle, thus making it more difficult for germs and fluid to collect in the middle ear.

During a cold, fluid accumulates in the middle ear. If the eustachian tube does not function properly and the fluid remains trapped, germs may cause an infection of the fluid within the cavity of the middle ear. The infected fluid accumulates behind the eardrum, presses on the eardrum, and produces intense pain. If the pressure from the trapped fluid builds up too much, this fluid may rupture the eardrum, and you may notice drainage of fluid outside the ear canal. This fluid resembles the secretions of a runny nose.

It is important for parents to be vigilant about recognizing the signs of a ruptured eardrum. Once the pressure is released, the eardrum ruptures, and the child feels better. But this is actually a false improvement; the infection still should be treated to allow the perforated area of the eardrum to heal. Continuous scarring of the eardrum can result in permanent hearing loss.

Ear infections often bother a child more at night. When she is lying down, the fluid presses down on her eardrum. A parent will often notice that his baby feels better when he holds her in an upright position or allows her to stand up in her crib.

How to recognize an ear infection in your child. The older child can tell you when his ear hurts, but it is often difficult for a parent to suspect an ear infection in a preverbal child. While some infants give no easily identifiable signs of ear infections, most show the following signs: your baby starts off with a clear, runny nose but is reasonably happy; the nasal discharge progresses from runny to thick; and your child's behavior moves from happy to increasingly cranky and irritable. Teething may be confused with ear infections, but when teething, your child should look generally well and his throat and nose secretions should not be persistently yellow or green. The combination of a discharging nose, with or without yellow drainage from the eyes, and increasing crankiness in the child should alert parents to the possibility of an ear infection, and a doctor should be consulted. Ear infections by themselves are not contagious. The child is contagious if he has a cold along with the ear infection.

Sometimes the fluid that builds up in the middle ear does not become infected and may not produce significant pain (this is called "serous otitis media"). This fluid will restrict the movement of the eardrum, thus diminishing your child's hearing. Even if only fluid is in the middle ear and there is no infection, most children show some change in behavior as a result of their diminishing hearing. This altered behavior may be the only sign to alert you of a middle ear problem.

How to prevent ear infections. Most children, because of the eustachian tube structure, will have occasional ear infections. The following suggestions may help lessen the frequency and severity of these infections.

1. Breastfeed your infant as long as possible. Breast-fed infants have fewer ear infections.
2. Control allergies. Allergies often cause fluid to build up in the middle ear, which can get infected. Food allergies, especially those caused by dairy products, and inhalant allergies, especially those caused by cigarette smoke and dust (such as that caused by stuffed animals in the bedroom), are the most common.
3. Observe your child's "cold pattern" and treat these colds early and appropriately. If your child has had previous ear infections and the usual sequence of events is first a runny nose, then a snotty nose, then crankiness, it may be wise to seek medical attention at the snotty-nose stage before the cold settles in your child's ears.

139

4. Some medications prevent the frequent occurrence of ear infection. Your doctor can recommend what is best for your child.

Treating ear infections. Most children can be grouped according to their type of ear infection: those with an occasional infection that clears up well with treatment; those with recurrent infections that need long-term treatment; and those with recurrent infections that do not respond to medical treatment but require surgical procedures.

The child with an occasional ear infection. After your doctor diagnoses an ear infection (otitis media), she will usually prescribe an antibiotic. The strength of the antibiotic and the duration it is to be taken will depend upon the severity of the infection and your child's past history of response to treatment. The healing of an ear infection usually goes through two phases. In the first phase your child should feel better within one or two days, and he may seem perfectly well within two or three days. During this time most of the germs have been killed by the antibiotic and the pressure of the fluid lessened somewhat so that your child's pain is nearly gone in the first few days. The second phase is that of gradual resolution of the fluid or drainage of this fluid from the middle ear through the eustachian tube. For this reason it is important to complete the prescribed duration of treatment. If you stop the antibiotics as soon as your child feels better, the remaining fluid in the middle ear may become reinfected, and the whole process must start all over again. It is also extremely important for your doctor to recheck your child's ear as soon as the prescribed antibiotic is finished. Your doctor may elect to continue a milder medication for a while longer if the infection is not gone completely. Partially treated ear infections are a common cause of permanent hearing deficits; therefore, follow-up checks are extremely important.

What can you do if your child awakens in the middle of the night with an earache? It is usually not necessary to phone your doctor immediately since antibiotics may take as long as twelve hours to have any effect and will not immediately relieve the pain. Try the following pain-relieving measures. Seat your child upright, and try to parent her back to sleep in that position. This often takes the pressure of the infected fluid off the eardrum and eases the pain. Warm some oil, such as olive oil, and squirt a few drops into the sore ear. Encourage your child to lie with the sore ear up, and pump the outer edge of the canal, trying to move the drops down toward the eardrum to relieve the pain. If your child has had frequent infections before, it is wise to keep an anesthetic ear drop for these middle-of-the-night earaches. Give him analgesics (aspirin or acetaminophen). These measures will often tide your child over until morning when you can consult your doctor, even though the child may seem to feel better by morning.

The child with recurrent ear infections. Some children have one ear infection after another, occurring every few weeks. Parents are usually frustrated by the continued recurrence of these infections and the continued medical expense. Although children are usually resilient to recurrent medical illnesses, children with recurrent ear infections often begin to show deteriorating behavior such as chronic irritability. I call this the "ear personality," which is common in children with recurrent ear infections simply because they do not feel well or hear well. One of the main changes parents notice after these recurrent ear infections are treated appropriately is that their children act better. Remember, a child who feels right usually acts right.

Parents take heart. There are ways to prevent these recurrent ear infections. The usual reason children have them is that the previous infection has never completely cleared up and the fluid remains behind the eardrum even though the germs have been treated appropriately with antibiotics. What usually happens is that the child has one ear infection and is treated for seven or ten days; he feels better, and then three or four weeks later he is back in the doctor's office with another ear infection because the fluid remained in the eardrum and became reinfected.

If your child's ear infections are occurring more frequently and lasting longer, your doctor may suggest a prevention regimen aimed at preventing the fluid from reaccumulating in the middle ear and at preventing the fluid that does accumulate from becoming infected. One such regimen consists of the following measures.

Strict allergy control. Your doctor may take a history to determine what possible allergens, such as dairy products, cigarette smoke, animal dander, or dust from dust-collecting stuffed animals, may be affecting your child. These allergens should be removed from your child's environment.

Eustachian tube exercises are designed to pop open the eustachian tubes and allow the accumulated fluid to drain. Eustachian tube exercises and strict allergy control are designed to keep the fluid from accumulating in the middle ear.

Daily medication. Usually a mild antibiotic keeps the fluid that does not drain from constantly becoming reinfected. These daily small doses of the mild antibiotic are often easier on a child's system than the periodic strong antibiotics.

This prevention regimen is extremely effective for the majority of children. Keeping a child free of ear infections for several months often allows the uninfected eustachian tube to grow properly and thus function properly; whereas, repeated infections further hinder the eustachian tube from functioning, which results in more infections, and the cycle continues. These prevention regimens are used for periods of three to six months, and thereafter your child is taken off the medications to see if the infection recurs. Most children indeed outgrow these recurrent ear infections by age five.

Surgical treatment. Occasionally a child will not respond to medical treatment of an ear infection. His middle ear will continue to have persistent fluid until it eventually becomes thick and gluelike, and it only can be removed by opening up the eardrum (called a "myringotomy") and draining out the fluid. Tiny plastic tubes are inserted surgically through the eardrums to allow the accumulated fluids to drain out, thus lessening the frequency of middle-ear infections and giving an immediate improvement in the child's hearing. In my experience, most children who have had their infections treated appropriately, who have been followed up appropriately, and who have been put on prevention regimens early and long enough have avoided surgical treatment.

At this point, let me caution parents against a common mistake in using the medical system. A child has a few ear infections, and a well-meaning friend or relative says, "Why don't you take your child to an ear specialist?" A better use of the current medical system both for you and your child is to stick with your child's physician who is trained primarily in the medical treatment of ear infections, is more familiar with childhood ear infections, and is less likely to recommend a surgical remedy. If your child has gone through the nonsurgical steps of treatment and the ear infections continue, your pediatrician then will refer you to an ear specialist. In this case the decision to administer surgical treatment for your child's ear infections is a combined decision between pediatrician and ear specialist, and your child will ultimately profit from this communication between his two doctors.

Parents, I cannot overemphasize the importance of being vigilant in treating your child's ear infections. Recurrent ear infections usually occur during a stage of speech development in the young child. If a child's hearing is lost periodically during these formative years of speech development, the child may show some speech delay and some permanent hearing loss. Even more noticeable are the chronic behavioral problems that occur with chronic ear infections. Poor school performance is also a common result of chronic ear infections in the older child.

Common Intestinal Problems

Some variations in children's stools are normal. The stools of a newly born baby contain a lot of swallowed amniotic fluid called "meconium," which accounts for the dark green, sticky, tarlike consistency. The newborn's stools are normally greenish brown for the first week or two, thereafter assuming a normal yellowish brown color. The stools of breast-fed babies tend to be of a yellow, mustard-like consistency, tend to be frequent, and have a buttermilk-like, nonoffensive odor. It is normal for stools to show an occasional green color. They may be persistently green if the child's formula contains added iron. A sick child with a persistently green stool that is also extremely runny and mucousy may have an intestinal infection.

The frequency and consistency of stools vary considerably from child to child. Some babies have four to six stools every day; others have one soft stool every three to five days. Intestinal problems in a child are nearly always manifested by some outward sign, such as paleness, pain, and poor weight gain. If your child is generally well, it is unlikely that she has any serious underlying intestinal problem even though her stools may seem unusual.

A change in diet is often accompanied by a change in stool consistency. Some formulas are more constipating than others. Rice and bananas tend to be constipating foods, whereas foods that tend to loosen the stools are corn syrup and most fruits and fruit juices, such as prunes or prune juice. It is common for stools to be loose during any condition that produces a lot of mucous in the throat, such as teething or a cold. Because antibiotics often change the kind of bacteria that normally reside in the intestines, it is common to have loose stools for a few weeks following a course of antibiotics.

Constipation refers to the consistency of the child's stools and difficulty in passing the stools, not to the frequency of the stools. Some infants and small children normally have bowel movements once every three to five days and if they do not appear uncomfortable, they are not constipated. A constipated baby draws his legs up onto a distended abdomen, strains, and becomes red in the face; he passes hard, pellet-like stools with much difficulty. Since the infant's rectum is often small, the passage of a hard stool may cause a small tear in the wall of the rectum called a "rectal fissure." This fissure may produce a few streaks of fresh blood on the stool or a few drops of blood on the diaper.

When your infant strains to pass a stool, insert a glycerin suppository (available at drugstores without prescription) high into his rectum. Hold his buttocks together for a few minutes so that the suppository can dissolve. These suppositories look like little rocket ships, and for the tiny baby, you may need to cut the suppository in half and insert the pointed top end. If one formula appears to be constipating, try a change of formula. Also, give your baby extra water. Constipation in the breastfeeding baby is seldom a problem. Some mothers have found that cheese in their diet somehow can cause hard stools in their babies through the breast milk. It *is* a common occurrence for breast-fed babies (older than two months) to have a bowel movement only once every three to seven days, and when the stool finally comes, it is not hard at all, but more like a major mudslide! Unless the baby is uncomfortable (most are not), you don't need to worry. If the stool is hard, or baby is uncomfortable, follow the advice given on the use of suppositories, prunes, and/or extra water. Adding a tablespoon of corn syrup to eight ounces of formula also may soften your infant's stools, but do not add it more than once or twice a day without first checking with your doctor. By three months of age a baby is old enough to add some pureed prunes or prune juice to his diet.

Constipation in the older child commonly causes recurrent abdominal pain. Busy children often ignore the urge to defecate, and they allow the stools to remain in the rectum until they get hard. Because a hard stool is usually a painful stool, children choose to ignore the painful stimulus and further increase their own constipation. The longer a child is constipated, the weaker the rectal muscles become and the less the urge to defecate becomes, creating a vicious and long-standing cycle of constipation. Older children (ages five to ten) who are chronically constipated often will soil their pants. This embarrassing problem often presents itself as a "diarrhea" problem but is in reality due to the leaking of stools from lower intestinal muscles that have been weakened by chronic constipation. Paradoxically, treating the child with soiled pants as a constipated child may resolve this embarrassing problem.

You may treat constipation in the older child by following these suggestions.

Teach your child to respond immediately to her urge-to-go signal, not to hold on to her stools. Explain to her that not following this signal weakens the "donut muscles" around the rectum and will eventually cause her to have pain when she has a bowel movement. (The muscle surrounding the opening from the bladder and the muscles surrounding the rectum do resemble a donut and your child can understand this analogy.)

Your doctor may prescribe stool softeners or laxatives before bedtime to encourage your child to have a bowel movement the next morning. Some naturally laxative foods include fruit, prune juice, corn syrup, vegetable roughage, and bran cereal. Potentially constipating foods are rice, cheese, bananas, and chocolate. Remember that it takes four to six weeks to treat chronic constipation. The stools need to remain soft for that length of time in order for the intestinal muscles to regain their strength.

Diarrhea, meaning "liquid stools," refers more to the consistency of the stools than to the frequency. Infants and children normally have prolonged periods of loose stools due to some conditions already mentioned. When should you worry about diarrhea? The most frequent cause of problem diarrhea in childhood is the intestinal infection *gastroenteritis,* usually caused by a virus. If the intestinal lining becomes infected, it heals very slowly. During the healing process, the enzymes in the intestinal lining that help digest and absorb food do not function properly. This results in stools that are very frequent, watery, explosive, green, mucousy, and foul smelling. This kind of diarrhea is usually accompanied by cold symptoms and a generally unwell child.

Diarrhea becomes a worrisome problem when it leads to *dehydration,* a condition in which your child loses more water and body salts than he takes in. Signs of dehydration in your child are obvious weight loss; dry eyes, dry skin, and dry mouth; diminishing urine output; an increasingly quiet child (called "lethargy"); and often fever. No matter how frequent and loose your child's stools seem to be, if he is happy, bright-eyed, has wet eyes and mouth, is urinating well, and has not lost weight, you do not have to worry.

Treatment of diarrhea. Your main goal in treating your child for diarrhea is to avoid dehydration. Decrease those foods that cannot be absorbed by infected intestines, and increase solutions containing extra salt and water, which your child loses in the diarrhea. The following suggestions will help you accomplish these goals.

Weigh your baby without her clothes on the most

accurate scale you can obtain. This is her baseline weight. Weigh her daily, preferably each morning before you feed her. If she has no significant weight loss, she is not becoming dehydrated. As a rough guide, if your child loses up to 5 percent of her baseline body weight (for example, a twenty-pound child loses one pound), she has experienced a significant amount of dehydration, and you should call your doctor immediately. Rapid weight loss should concern you more than slow and gradual weight loss. A twenty-pound infant's losing a pound of body weight over a period of two days is a much greater concern than his losing the same amount of weight over a period of two weeks. Infants usually appear very sick with a rapid weight loss but do not usually appear that sick if the weight loss has been slow and gradual.

Stop all solid food, dairy products, and formulas made with cow's milk. If you are breastfeeding, it is rarely necessary to stop even temporarily, since human milk is not nearly as irritating to infected intestines as cow's milk products. This is true also if your child is vomiting. Breast milk is easy on the stomach and nursing is comforting.

Give your child a clear fluid diet. These fluids should contain simple sugars, which are easy to digest in order to provide calories, and salts, which your child is losing in the diarrhea fluid. Make a sugar solution by adding one level tablespoon of ordinary table sugar to eight ounces of boiled water (do not boil the sugar solution because boiling may cause the water to evaporate and make the solution too strong). Flat ginger ale and colas are readily available sources of sugars. Fluids containing a lot of salt are called "oral electrolyte solutions" (Pedialyte, Lytren, and Infalyte are available at your pharmacy or grocery store without prescription). Do not continue these electrolyte solutions for more than twenty-four hours without checking with your physician. The sips-and-chips method of administering fluids provides your child small, frequent feedings (two ounces at a time) rather than a large feeding. In the older infant this is accomplished best by frequent sips of fluid and ice chips or juice Popsicles. A clear fluid diet alone should not be continued more than forty-eight hours without checking with your physician, since this kind of diet continued too long may itself produce diarrhea, called "starvation stools."

After twenty-four to forty-eight hours, if your child is not losing weight and the diarrhea has lessened somewhat, add semi-solid foods such as rice cereal without milk and mashed bananas. Continue the regimen of small, frequent fluid feedings. As the stools continue to improve, gradually add applesauce, saltine crackers, gelatin, and yogurt. As your child's stools become more solid, so can his diet.

Resume milk or formula very gradually and only after you have seen much improvement in your child's condition. Resume the formula by diluting it to half regular strength. Gradually return to the regular strength over the next several days. Do not boil milk or give undiluted skim milk to a child who has diarrhea since these solutions are too concentrated and may worsen the dehydration.

If the diarrhea worsens after you have gone back to dairy products, go back a few steps and begin the regimen all over again. For a formula-fed child who is recovering from diarrhea, a soybean-based formula is often tolerated better than a formula made with cow's milk. Following an intestinal infection, it is normal to have a prolonged period of loose stools (I call this "nuisance diarrhea"), which may last for several weeks or months. This is because the intestinal lining is very slow to heal in most children. If your child has persistent diarrhea, it is more important to focus on the total child than only on his bottom. If your child appears generally well and is not continuing to lose weight, you do not need to worry even though his stools remain loose.

When to call your doctor about diarrhea. After you have followed these steps and your child continues to lose weight, show signs of dehydration, be in increasing pain, or look increasingly ill, call you doctor for more advice. Before making your call, have the following information available: the frequency and characteristics of the stools; the degree of weight loss and over what period of time; details about any associated symptoms such as vomiting, fever, signs of a cold or increasing pain, or any signs of dehydration; and what kind of treatment you have been giving. Parents, do not be disappointed if your doctor decides not to administer medication to attempt to stop your child's diarrhea. Most diarrhea in childhood is best treated by dietary restriction and time. Narcotic medications, which are often used to control diarrhea in adults, are generally not safe for children.

Besides these methods of treatment, much prayer and patience are needed to cope with diarrhea in a young child, because this problem is usually a long-term nuisance. Vomiting and diarrhea occurring together are more worrisome than if one occurs without the other.

Vomiting in the young infant. Most vomiting in the first few months is simply regurgitation (spitting up) resulting from a temporary feeding problem, such as air-swallowing or overfeeding. This vomiting is not usually a medical problem and usually subsides when the infant sits upright, when he is between six and eight months. Milk allergy is also a cause of vomiting in the young infant.

Vomiting in the older infant and child is caused most often by an infection or an irritation of the stomach, called "gastritis." This condition is often accompanied by nausea, stomachache, and retching (dry heaves).

There are more serious causes of vomiting. In the tiny infant, projectile vomiting (vomitus coming out under great force for several feet), which persists with nearly every feeding and is accompanied by signs of weight loss, may indicate a condition called "pyloric stenosis." This condition occurs primarily in male infants two months of age and is due to the lower end of the stomach's being too narrow for food to pass through. The sudden onset of vomiting in a generally ill-appearing child, persistent green bile vomitus, accompanied by severe abdominal pain are signs that the intestines are twisted and obstructed. These conditions are surgical emergencies and require immediate medical attention.

How to assess and treat the vomiting child. If your child's vomiting is associated with other symptoms, such as severe abdominal pain, signs of cold, high fever, headaches, or increasing drowsiness, it is probably due to a temporary intestinal infection that can be treated by methods similar to those described in the section on diarrhea. Prevent dehydration by replacing the fluids he loses in his vomitus. Use the sips-and-chips method of fluid replacement. Popsicles made with frozen apple juice, flat ginger ale, or cola are the best means of getting fluids into an infant or a child very slowly. Popsicles also may be made with the oral electrolyte solutions described earlier. The sips-and-chips method allows the small, frequent feedings necessary if the intestinal lining of the stomach is infected. Allowing fluid intake in more than small, slow amounts can cause rebound vomiting, resulting in more electrolyte loss. Breastfeeding can continue.

Follow the same guidelines described under the section on diarrhea for noting signs of dehydration and for knowing when to call your doctor. Antivomiting medications are usually not effective in children. As with the treatment of diarrhea, mainly diet restriction and fluid replacement will prevent dehydration in the vomiting child.

Infectious Childhood Diseases

Since children are socially oriented, they tend to share infectious diseases. The following chart will help you identify these illnesses and treat them appropriately.

	Characteristic Features	Treatment and Precautions
Measles (red measles)	■ begins like common cold: runny nose; severe cough; reddened eyes, sensitive to light ■ high fever (104°), lasts 5 days ■ rash: purplish-red, raised, begins on face,	■ contagious from onset of symptoms until end of rash ■ preventable by vaccine ■ treatment: fever control, comforting measures

Infectious Childhood Diseases *(Cont'd)*

	Characteristic Features	Treatment and Precautions
Measles (*red measles*) Cont'd	spreads to entire body, begins at height of fever, lasts 5 days	
German measles (*rubella*)	▪ low fever (101°), mild cold ▪ rash: pinkish-red, faint, disappears by third day ▪ swollen glands behind neck ▪ differs from red measles: child not very sick, lower fever, fainter rash, less cough	▪ contagious from a week before rash to 5 days after rash gone ▪ preventable by vaccine ▪ avoid exposure to pregnant women ▪ treatment: comforting measures
Mumps	▪ begins as flu-like illness ▪ neck glands beneath earlobe markedly swollen and tender ▪ low fever (101°), headache, nausea	▪ contagious from onset of symptoms until swelling gone ▪ preventable by vaccine ▪ treatment: comforting measures
Roseola	▪ usually affects babies between 9 and 18 months of age ▪ sudden onset of high fever (103°–105°) in previously well baby	▪ not considered a serious illness ▪ no vaccine ▪ not highly contagious ▪ treatment: comforting measures

	Characteristic Features	Treatment and Precautions
Roseola Cont'd	■ lasts 3 days ■ baby "not very sick" ■ rash: rose-pink, faint, appears after fever gone, lasts 24 hours	
Chicken pox	■ low fever (101°–102°), generally unwell feeling ■ rash: initially may appear on trunk as tiny dots resembling bites, rapidly progresses to blister-like vesicles on red bases; new crops appear rapidly as old ones form a crust	■ contagious from 2 days before rash until all vesicles crusted over ■ vaccine: available for special patients ■ treatment: comforting measures
Scarlet fever	■ sunburn-like, red rash ■ fever (103°) and sick child ■ sore throat, swollen neck glands ■ tongue white-coated or strawberry red ■ same as strep throat with a rash ■ rash: rose-pink, faint	■ cause: streptococcus ■ contagious for 24–48 hours after antibiotics begun ■ treatment: antibiotics

■ SIDS: Reducing the Worry; Reducing the Risk

Each year six thousand babies in the United States go to sleep and never wake up. No one knows why. Sudden Infant Death Syndrome (SIDS) is the primary cause of death in infants between one month and one year, with peak incidence around three months of age. While these unexplained stop-breathing episodes occur in only 1 out of every 1,000 babies, SIDS ranks near the top of every parent's worry list.

But there's good news. Recent research strongly indicates a number of practical measures that parents can take to lower the risk and worry of SIDS. These risk-reduction measures enhance a baby's pre- and postnatal development, promote respiratory health, and increase a mother's awareness of her baby's needs—all of which can reduce the likelihood of Sudden Infant Death Syndrome.

Provide a Healthy Womb Environment

Premature birth and low birthweight are two of the highest risk factors for SIDS. To give your baby the best prenatal start:

- *Get good prenatal care.* Babies whose mothers receive little or no prenatal care are at highest risk of preterm birth.
- *Eat right.* Good nutrition during pregnancy feeds your baby right.
- *Avoid cigarettes and drugs.* Exposure to these harmful substances during pregnancy

decreases the oxygen supply to developing tissues. This can harm the part of the baby's brain that regulates breathing. The risk of SIDS increases eightfold in infants of substance-abusing mothers. Researchers believe that drugs such as opiates and cocaine constrict blood vessels in the placenta, reducing oxygen supply to the preborn baby. As a result, a baby's cardiorespiratory control centers may develop abnormally and are more likely to fail.

Another Good Reason to Breastfeed

Breastfeeding has long been cited as an important factor in a baby's overall health and development. Studies indicate a lower incidence of SIDS in breast-fed babies. Here are possible reasons why:

- Breast milk enhances neurological development—helping the respiratory control center of the brain develop.
- Nutrients in breast milk fight infections that could harm a baby's respiratory health.
- Breastfeeding reduces gastroesophageal reflux, which can cause stop-breathing episodes.
- Breast-fed babies are more easily aroused from sleep, which may be a SIDS-reduction factor.
- Breastfeeding improves breathing and swallowing coordination.
- Nursing stimulates maternal hormones that increase a mother's awareness of her baby.

No Smoking, Please

Studies show that exposure to cigarette smoke at least doubles the risk of SIDS, and heavy maternal smoking—more than twenty cigarettes a day—increases the risk fivefold.

Even passive smoking can increase the risk of SIDS. Suppose you were about to take your baby into a room when you noticed the following sign posted on the door: *Warning! This room contains poisonous gases that have been linked to cancer and lung damage and are especially harmful to the breathing passages of young infants.* You certainly wouldn't take your baby in there! But that's exactly what happens when your baby spends time in a room frequented by smokers.

Smoking interferes with the development of the cardiorespiratory control centers in a baby's brain. In addition, smoke paralyzes the cilia—tiny filaments that clear mucous from the air passages—compromising a baby's breathing. And mothers who smoke have lower levels of prolactin, the hormone that regulates milk production. Prolactin deficiency may lead to diminished maternal awareness of and responsiveness to an infant's needs.

Sleep Safely

The sleeping environment you provide for your infant also plays a significant role in reducing the risk of SIDS.

- Put baby to sleep on her back rather than her tummy. Studies show that back-sleeping has decreased the risk of SIDS by as much as

50 percent in some countries. Babies' arousability from sleep—an infant's built-in protective mechanism—works better when babies sleep on their backs. A baby sleeping face-down may press her head into the mattress, forming a pocket of air around her face. As a result, she rebreathes exhaled air that has diminished oxygen.

- Avoid putting baby to sleep on unsafe surfaces, such as beanbag chairs or couches.
- Do not sleep with your baby if you are under the influence of any drug or alcohol that diminishes your sensitivity to your baby's presence.
- Avoid overheating your baby during sleep.

Whether sleeping with your baby lowers the risk of SIDS is a controversial issue, but we believe that safe sleep-sharing is a powerful SIDS risk-reduction factor. Current research suggests that SIDS is a defect in the normal arousability from sleep, so it's common sense that any sleeping arrangement that increases baby's arousability and mother's awareness would lower the risk of SIDS. This is exactly what sleep-sharing does.

The good news is that SIDS is no longer considered to be a mysterious cloud that hangs over a baby's crib waiting to snatch her last breath. While there is no guaranteed protection against Sudden Infant Death Syndrome, taking these practical steps can reduce the risk and worry of losing a baby to it. ■

Common Childhood Emergencies

Because children are active and curious, they are subject to bumps and scrapes. Be familiar with the following information to respond effectively in the event of a medical emergency.

Poisoning

If your child swallows a potentially poisonous substance, the following emergency steps should be followed:

Step 1. Call your local poison control center. Their phone number may be found by consulting your local hospital or in the yellow pages. It would be wise to display the phone number of the poison control center in a conspicuous place such as on your telephone.

Step 2. If advised by the poison control center, encourage your child to drink lots of water to dilute the poison.

Step 3. Keep syrup of *ipecac* in your medicine cabinet. This syrup is very effective for inducing vomiting, thereby removing the potentially harmful substance. If advised to induce vomiting by your poison control center, give your child one tablespoon (three teaspoons) of syrup of ipecac in eight ounces of water or noncarbonated fruit juice. If vomiting does not occur within twenty minutes, give one more tablespoon of ipecac in juice or water. Be prepared for the vomiting by keeping your child in the bathroom or outside for forty-five minutes after the first dose of ipecac. It is important not to induce vomiting before consulting the poison control center because certain poisons may be harmful if vomiting is induced, and some substances may not require vomiting at all.

Head Injury

God anticipated busy children would sustain many falls and knocks to the head during the normal process of growing up. For this reason He provided the skull as a helmet to protect the brain. The scalp is also subject to head injuries. Because the scalp is very rich in blood vessels, even a small cut on the scalp bleeds profusely. Also, blows to the scalp may break the underlying blood vessels, producing a large swelling called a "goose-egg."

First-aid steps for head injuries: (1) If your child has a cut or swelling, apply an ice pack and pressure for at least twenty minutes. This usually stops the bleeding and will reduce the size of the eventual goose egg. (2) Lay your child down in a comfortable place and begin a period of observation. If there is an underlying brain injury, it takes time for the swelling or bleeding in the brain to produce signs of internal pressure. The signs of a brain injury may not develop for several hours. Observe your child for the following steps.

1. *Is your child alert?* Is he responding to simple questions? Does he seem aware of his name, where he is, where he lives, the names of Mommy and Daddy and brothers and sisters? Be prepared for your child's wanting to go to sleep after a head injury since sleep is the usual refuge of consolation for an injured child. Let your child fall asleep, but observe him every couple of hours for any change in breathing patterns or skin color. It is wise to wake your child every two hours at least to check his eyes and his balance.

2. *Can your child look at you straight in the eye?* The eyes are the mirror of the brain, especially in a head injury. If your child looks at you straight in the eye, if

his pupils are the same size in both eyes, and if he can see objects clearly, he is not likely to have an underlying brain injury. Ask your child to cover one eye and count how many fingers he sees. If he complains of seeing double, you have cause for concern.

3. *Is your child vomiting persistently?* It is normal for children to vomit once or twice after a blow to the head; therefore, it is wise to feed your child only clear fluids following the injury. If your child shows persistent vomiting, even of clear fluids, your doctor should be called.

4. *Is your child walking steadily?* If your child is off balance, especially if he is exhibiting weakness in one arm or leg, contact your doctor.

5. *Does your child have headaches?* Some headaches are to be expected after a blow to the head, and they usually subside within a few hours. If your child's headaches increase in severity—especially if they are accompanied by some of the signs we have discussed—call your doctor. Do not give aspirin for head injuries since it may increase the bleeding. Acetaminophen is the preferred analgesic.

When should you call your doctor? If any of these five signs occurs, call your doctor immediately or take your child to your hospital. If none of the signs are apparent, you may wish to check with your doctor shortly after the accident for further instructions. If these signs of brain injury are not present, you do not need to rush your child to a hospital for skull X rays. A period of careful observation and a medical examination are more useful than skull X rays. Your doctor will advise you as to whether skull X rays are necessary.

Choking

Infants and small children like to "mouth" small objects which can get caught in their throats and obstruct their breathing. Try the following procedure if your child starts choking.

Step 1. If your child can talk, cry, or cough, her airway is not obstructed and you should not interfere with her own efforts to dislodge the material. If your child is breathing normally and is not panicky, give her emotional support and allow her cough reflex to expel the object.

Step 2. If your child cannot speak or cry, is having difficulty getting air, is blue, or is losing consciousness, position her head-down and apply four hard blows to her back between the shoulder blades. If the blows to the back do not dislodge the object, administer four chest thrusts: with your child lying on her back on the floor, place your hands alongside the lower rib cage on both sides and quickly compress the chest downward and upward with the thrusts of your arms. If the chest-thrust procedure does not dislodge the object, repeat the four back blows.

Step 3. While administering step 2, call to someone to summon the paramedics. It is wise to have your local paramedics' number displayed conspicuously on every phone in the house. In most metropolitan cities the paramedic system is tied in with a simple 911, making it unnecessary to take time to look up a number. In many cities, the 911 system is automatically tied into a computer that gives the paramedics the name and location of the dialing phone. It is wise to check periodically to see if the 911 emergency system is operating in your community.

The Heimlich maneuver is another procedure for dislodging an object caught in the airway of a choking person. Most authorities recommend the combination of back blows and chest thrusts in infants because of the possible damage to abdominal organs with the Heimlich maneuver. For older children over three years the Heimlich maneuver is preferable and is performed as follows: stand behind the choking person and wrap your arms around her waist, making a fist with one hand and grasping the fist with the other. Place the thumb side of your fist toward the upper abdomen and compress with a quick upward thrust, repeating several times if necessary. This abdominal pressure is transmitted to the lungs, compressing the lungs and pushing the object up out of the airway.

It is not wise to use your finger to dislodge the object from the back of the child's throat unless you can see the object and are certain you can get your finger around it. Inserting a large finger in a child's small throat may push the object farther back into the throat or may cause the child to panic and suck the object into her lungs.

Swallowed Objects

Children are prone to swallow small objects such as coins. Most of these pass into the intestines and are eliminated in twenty-four to forty-eight hours without causing harm. Occasionally, objects such as a coin or hard candy may lodge in the child's esophagus, causing excessive drooling (because the child cannot swallow his saliva) and pain in the area where the object has become stuck. If these signs occur in your child, take him to the hospital or call your doctor for advice.

Convulsions

Most convulsions in a previously well child less than five years old are caused by fever and are called "febrile convulsions." These convulsions usually stop when you lower the fever by undressing your child and placing him in a tepid bath (see pages 126–33 for ways to lower your child's fever). As long as he is breathing well and is not blue during these febrile convulsions, your child's shaking arms and legs do not harm him, and the shaking will gradually subside as the fever is lowered.

If your child stops breathing during a convulsion, is foaming at the mouth, or turning blue, place him in the prone position with his head down, allowing the secretions to drain out of his throat and his tongue to fall forward. This clears your child's airway, allowing him to breathe during the convulsion. If your child is showing signs of breathing difficulty during the convulsion, paramedics should be called immediately.

Burns

If your child is burned, the following emergency steps will lessen the pain and severity of the burn.

1. Immediately submerge the burned area in cold water for at least twenty minutes. Do not use ice packs or bare ice cubes on the burn since these may increase the damage to the tissue caused by the burn.
2. Cover the burned area with a clean cloth soaked in cold water until the pain of the burn subsides. Do not apply butter or oils.
3. Take your child to the hospital or call your doctor for advice on continued care of the burn.

Besides the above first-aid measure to alleviate the pain and minimize skin damage, the following suggestions will lessen the cosmetic scarring of the burned area.

1. Keep the burn covered with an appropriate antibiotic ointment, such as silvadene, prescribed by your doctor.
2. Do not break the blisters without your doctor's advice.
3. Wash the burned area twice a day under a jet of water such as a tap or shower and dry thoroughly with a clean cloth.
4. To prevent contracture of the burned area if the burn is over a flexion crease (such as the palm of the hand or the wrist), frequent stretching of the burned area should be encouraged.
5. As the burned area is healing, your doctor may need to remove some of the dead tissue to minimize infection. Some burns heal better with the open method (washed frequently and covered with an appropriate antibiotic ointment but without a dressing), and others need to be covered with a dressing. Your doctor will advise you which method of treatment is necessary.

Nosebleeds

Most nosebleeds in children are due to nose picking and injury to the tiny blood vessels lining the inside of the nostrils. They are more common in the wintertime, especially in homes with central heating, because the low humidity causes the inside of the nose to dry. If your child is prone to nosebleeds, running a humidifier or vaporizer during the months requiring central heating may be necessary.

Apply the following first-aid measures during a nosebleed.

Apply a ball of wet cotton into the bleeding nostril and pinch the nostrils together. Also, apply pressure for ten minutes to the upper lip just below the nostrils. This compresses the major blood vessel supplying the nose. Seat your child leaning slightly forward. After the nosebleed stops, leave the piece of cotton lodged in your child's nostril for several hours and then very gently remove the piece of cotton, being careful not to dislodge the clot and cause the bleeding to recur. If using these measures does not stop your child's nosebleed, call your doctor or take your child to the hospital.

Nose Injuries

The nose contains tiny, soft bones and acts like a shock absorber which protects against jarring of the underlying brain. Nasal bones are easily fractured, and the following emergency measures will minimize cosmetic and functional impairment from a blow to the nose. Apply an ice pack to the area of swelling for at least a half hour following the trauma. After this, if your child can breathe easily through both nostrils and if the nose is not crooked, the nose is likely to heal well without the fracture's having to be set. If signs of breathing obstruction or cosmetic distortion are present, consult your doctor immediately.

Interrupted Breathing

Step 1. After calling 911, clear your child's mouth of any secretions or foreign bodies (see entry on choking in this section).

167

Step 2. Employ mouth-to-mouth breathing. Place your child on his back and slightly bend his neck forward and his head backward in the so-called sniffing position. This is best attempted by kneeling alongside your child and placing one hand under his neck and the other on his forehead.

Fit your mouth snugly around your child's lips and nose. If your child is too large for you to make a good seal over his mouth and nose, pinch his nose and seal his mouth only. For a tiny baby, give four quick, gentle puffs (a puff is about the amount of air you can hold in your cheeks). For an older child, give enough air to make his chest rise. Apply a breath every two to three seconds. Continue the mouth-to-mouth breathing until your child resumes breathing himself or until trained help arrives.

I strongly advise all parents and expectant parents to take a CPR course from their local Red Cross.

Praying for Your Child

If you have selected a Christian physician and your child has a particularly disturbing medical problem, ask your physician to pray with you for your child. This practice gives your child total Christian medical care. We are given clear instruction on how to pray for healing in James 5:14–15.

Attending to the medical and physical needs of your child is but one aspect of parenting. Helping your child to sleep well and deciding whether or not to return to work and then successfully making that adjustment are made easier when the principles of attachment parenting are applied.

Part 3

Practical Parenting

CHAPTER 8

NIGHTTIME
PARENTING

■ "Lord, please give me one full night's sleep" is a common plea of an exhausted new parent. How to cope with night waking is probably one of the most common problems new parents face. This problem is frustrating for both parents and doctors. It's frustrating for the doctor who has no answer for how to get *all* children to sleep every night. It's frustrating for the parents who plea, "I've tried everything, and nothing works." Difficult problems do not have quick and easy answers, but there are some suggestions to help parents have realistic expectations of how babies sleep (or don't sleep) and to help both you and your baby get enough sleep.

Babies' Sleep Patterns

Just as there are wide variations in babies' personalities, there are wide variations in babies' sleep patterns. It is important for you to approach parenting with no expectations, no preconceived images of what a baby

171

should be like, especially about how he should sleep. One tired mother shared with me: "Before our baby came, I thought that all newborn babies did was eat and sleep. All my baby did was eat."

Early in their parenting career, preferably before the birth of their baby, I advise parents to pray an acceptance prayer frequently asking God to guide them in accepting whatever temperament their baby is blessed with and to give them the energy to parent according to the needs of their child. Some parents are blessed with easy sleepers (we have never had one, but I hear about them); other parents are blessed with frequent wakers. In both cases, the parents are blessed to have their child as he is.

You also need to be open to adjusting your parenting style to your baby's needs. If you approach your nighttime parenting with the same style of openness previously discussed, you and your baby will eventually sleep well and, more importantly, will feel right about it. If you approach your nighttime parenting determined to make your baby fit into a sleep pattern you feel he or she ought to have, you will experience many frustrating and sleepless nights.

Have Realistic Expectations of How Babies Sleep (or Don't Sleep)

Babies' sleep patterns differ from those of adults. Babies don't sleep through the night; they get their days and nights mixed up. They awaken frequently for feedings. One of the first facts of parenting life that new parents should know is that babies do what they do because God designed them that way.

When people fall asleep, they progress through many stages of sleep, from a very light sleep to a very deep sleep. To simplify the explanation, sleep can be divided into two stages: (1) light sleep and (2) deep sleep. Most adults spend the greatest percentage of their sleep time in deep sleep while babies spend most of their sleep time in light sleep.

If you watch your baby sleeping, you can identify easily which state of sleep he or she is in. In a state of light sleep, which is the more active sleep, babies appear to sleep although they are squirming, their breathing movements are somewhat irregular, and sometimes their eyes are only partially closed. If you lifted their eyelids, you would notice that their eyeballs were often moving. In fact, this state of light or active sleep is called "REM," or rapid eye movement sleep. When babies are in a state of deep sleep, their body is much quieter, and they are not easily aroused.

Since your baby is most easily awakened during this period of light sleep, one of the goals of parenting your baby to sleep is to minimize the arousal stimuli during that time. The first few months the average baby sleeps fourteen to eighteen hours per day, but that is not true for every baby. The sleep pattern of tiny babies resembles their feeding patterns—small, frequent feedings and short, frequent naps.

In their first three months, babies' sleeping states are poorly organized because, at that age, the concept of day and night has little meaning to them. A realistic expectation of nighttime parenting is for parents to organize their lifestyles and sleep styles around their baby's. The mother is advised to sleep during the day when the baby sleeps. In the first months, it is much more realistic, especially for the mother, to "sleep like a baby" than to expect the baby to sleep like an adult. As your baby gets older and his or her developing brain becomes capable of inhibiting arousal stimuli, the relative percentage of his deep sleep increases, usually reaching adult levels within two years.

Infants Go to Sleep Differently

Not only are infants' sleep patterns different from those of adults, but their way of going to sleep differs. Adults can "crash" rather quickly. Adults can go directly from the awake state into the state of deep sleep without passing through the initial period of REM or light sleep. Infants cannot do this. They enter sleep through an initial period of light sleep (lasting about twenty or thirty minutes), then enter a period of transitional sleep, and then drift into deep or non-REM sleep. If an arousal stimulus occurs during the initial light sleep, a baby will awaken easily because he never reached the deep-sleep phase. This pattern accounts for the difficult-to-settle baby about whom mothers often state, "He has to be fully asleep before he can be put down."

As babies mature, they begin to go directly to the state of deep sleep. They settle more quickly; they can be put down to go to sleep. This difference in sleep entry explains why infants need to be parented to sleep, not just put to bed to fall asleep on their own. They need to be nursed or rocked to sleep and gentled through this initial phase of light sleep. One of the arts of nighttime parenting is learning how to induce sleep in your baby by gentling him through the REM.

Why Your Baby Doesn't Sleep Through the Night

Throughout the night people experience peaks and valleys of light and deep sleep, or sleep cycles. The adult sleep cycle is about twice as long as an infant's (ninety minutes compared to forty-five to fifty minutes). The vulnerable period for night waking is during the transition from deep sleep into light sleep. Since babies have more of these transitions because their sleep cycles are shorter, they are more likely to wake up frequently during the night. One of the ways to minimize night waking, as shall be covered later, is to gentle your infant during these vulnerable periods.

Babies settle more easily as they get older. *Settling* means getting off to sleep easily and staying asleep through the night. The age at which babies settle and their number of hours of straight, uninterrupted sleep vary tremendously from baby to baby. In sleep studies, settling is defined as sleeping from midnight to 5:00 A.M. Expecting a baby under one year of age to sleep through the night from 8:00 P.M. to 8:00 A.M. is unrealistic.

If you are blessed with a somnolent baby, consider this a luxury. As your infant gets older, he or she undergoes what is called "sleep maturity" when the percentage of light sleep decreases and deep sleep increases, and the vulnerable periods of night waking lessen. Some studies show that about 70 percent of babies settle by three months and 90 percent by one year. Ten percent of babies never sleep uninterruptedly during the first two years. Even those babies who settle well may continue to have periodic night waking.

Toward the end of the first year, as your baby's brain becomes more capable of blocking arousal stimuli, both you and your baby will probably enjoy a brief period of an uninterrupted night's sleep. However, just as you feel your baby has kicked the night-waking habit, he or she may begin waking up again. Some children will go to sleep easily and stay asleep; some go to sleep with difficulty but stay asleep; some go to sleep easily but do not stay asleep; and some children want neither to go to sleep nor stay asleep. Fears, separation anxieties, disturbing dreams, and nightmares are the main stimuli for night waking of children from one to three years.

Why Some Infants Are Not Easy Sleepers

Parents, be assured that the maturity of your baby's sleep pattern is not a reflection of your parenting. A baby's sleep pattern often reflects his basic temperament. This may come as a surprise to some parents, but even-tempered babies enjoy a larger percentage of deep sleep. Children who exhibit very active temperaments during the day usually have a higher degree of restlessness and squirming activity during sleep. These high-need babies seem to carry their waking personalities into their sleep, having shorter periods of deep sleep and more frequent night waking. On the surface this would seem to be a mismatch of temperaments and sleep patterns. You would think that the more active babies would need more sleep (at least their parents do). I believe the reason for this paradox is that high-need babies do not have a well-developed stimulus barrier during the day or night.

Night waking may be of divine design. The longer I practice pediatrics and the more children my wife and I have, the more I learn to respect the fact that babies do what they do because they are designed that way. Babies do not awaken to annoy or to exhaust the parents on purpose. I feel that God may have designed frequent night waking for young babies for two reasons: (1) survival benefits and (2) developmental benefits.

Night waking may be a survival benefit. In the first few months, the infant's needs are highest, but his or her ability to communicate these needs is lowest. Suppose your baby had your sleep patterns and enjoyed more deep sleep than light sleep so that he or she was not easily aroused. If he or she became hungry and needed food, he or she might not awaken; if he or she got cold and needed warmth, he or she might not awaken; if his or her nose were plugged and his or her breathing compromised, he or she might not awaken. I feel that a baby's sleep patterns are part of the divine design for the survival of the young of the species in order that the infant may be allowed a state of awareness in which to communicate his or her survival needs.

Night waking may have developmental benefits. Some prominent sleep researchers theorize that the predominance of light sleep during the first year is important for development of the baby's brain. During the state of light sleep, the brain continues to operate; whereas, during the state of deep sleep the higher brain centers shut off, and the baby operates on the lower brain centers. The theory is that during the stage of most rapid brain growth (the first year), the brain needs to continue functioning during sleep in order to continue developing. As brain development gradually slows down, the infant has less light sleep and more deep sleep. (I have summarized the pertinent scientific studies relating to children's sleep in my book *Nighttime Parenting,* 1987, published by New American Library, New York.)

If tired parents have faith that God has indeed designed babies according to some nighttime plan that has both survival and developmental benefits, they may better accept their nighttime parenting. One day in the office I was consoling a tired mother by offering her the explanation of why frequent night waking may be

177

in accordance with God's design for development of her infant's brain. She responded, "In that case, he's going to be very smart."

Although frequent night waking may be according to God's design for some babies, I also feel that persistent fatigue in both babies and parents may not be. For this reason, I feel that part of the divine plan for nighttime parenting is that parents have the ability to help the baby organize his or her sleep patterns. I firmly believe that God would not have designed a baby with a sleep pattern too difficult for the parents to cope with. Tired parents and tired babies simply do not enjoy the relationship God has intended. For this reason, the following sections offer tips on how to help your baby organize his or her sleep patterns and how to widen your acceptance level and survive your baby's nighttime needs.

Sharing Sleep

One of the earliest decisions for nighttime parenting, and one that is very important to helping your baby organize his or her sleep pattern, concerns where your baby should sleep. Quite honestly, I feel that whatever sleeping arrangement gets all three of you the most sleep and leaves all three of you feeling right is the right sleeping arrangement for your individual family. What works for one family may not work for another.

Sharing sleep is an arrangement whereby you welcome your baby into your bed early in infancy and allow him or her to remain until he or she can sleep alone comfortably. Many Christian parents are confused about the conflicting opinions on this subject. They ask, "Is it all right for our baby to sleep with us?"

This section will present reasons why it is good to sleep with your baby and why it may in fact be according to God's design. My opinion, one that I have formed after much prayer and experience, both personal and professional, is that God intended the young of each species to sleep in close contact with the mother until the baby can comfortably sleep independently. I have advocated the concept of sharing sleep in my pediatric practice for the last twelve years, and we have practiced this arrangement in our own family. It is beautiful! It works! Perhaps this sleeping arrangement does not work for all families at all times, but in my experience it works for most families most of the time, provided it is done with the attitude that God has intended. The baby's sleeping close to or with the parents is a part of the natural continuum from mother's womb to mother's breasts to parents' bed, and weaning from all three places of security should occur only when mother and baby are ready.

The concept of sharing sleep is more an attitude than a decision about where your baby sleeps. It is an attitude of acceptance and mutual trust whereby an infant trusts his or her parents as a continually available support resource during the night just as the infant trusts them during the day. It is an attitude of trust for the parents, too, in that they trust what feels right in parenting their child rather than accept the cultural norms of the country or yield to the dictates of peer pressure. It is often difficult for new parents to listen to and accept the cues of their child about what type of care he or she needs. This is usually because of the many unfounded cultural taboos that have hampered intuitive child rearing and because of the unreasonable fear that they don't want their child to manipulate them.

Be open to accepting whatever sleeping arrangement works for your family. If all three of you sleep better with your baby in your bed and you all feel right about it, this arrangement is best for your family. This sleeping arrangement is sometimes called "the family bed." I prefer to call it "sharing sleep" because that implies more than sharing just a *place* to sleep; it also means that parents and babies share sleep cycles and attitudes about sleep.

Help Baby Organize His Sleep Patterns

The previous section established that babies have a vulnerable period for waking up as they pass from deep sleep into light sleep. Since they have these sleep-cycle changes every hour, babies are vulnerable to waking up as often as once every hour. Sleeping with a familiar, predictable person helps baby settle through this vulnerable period and resettle into the next stage of sleep before he or she is able to awaken fully.

In the first year, babies do not have object permanency. When something is out of sight, it is out of mind. Most babies under a year old do not have the ability to conceive Mother as existing somewhere else. When babies awaken alone, their aloneness may keep them from resettling into the next stage of sleep without awakening with a stressful cry.

When adults awaken from sleep, they wake in various states of confusion, but they usually can drift into the next state of sleep without becoming fully awake because they know where they are. The security of knowing where they are is often provided by a familiar somebody next to them. For a baby, waking up to a familiar attachment person often smoothes the transition from one state of sleep to the next and may keep him or her from waking fully or at least help him or her resettle into the next state of sleep without a great deal of separation anxiety.

When I wake in the morning and gaze upon the contented face of our "sleeping beauty," I can tell when she is passing through this vulnerable period because she often reaches out and touches one of us. When she reaches her anticipated target, a smile appears, and an "I'm okay" expression radiates from her face. Her eyes remain closed, and she often does not fully awaken. This advantage of nighttime parenting can only be realized by being open to your child at night.

Mothers Sleep Better

Parents, you may be surprised to discover that not only does baby sleep better when sharing sleep, but you do too. The reason for this may be summarized by one word—*harmony*. Just as it is important to achieve harmony with your child during the day, sleeping with your baby at night allows this harmony to continue so that baby and mother get their sleep cycles in sync with each other.

When this harmony is achieved, babies awaken their mothers during their mutual light-sleep cycles and sleep during their mutual deep-sleep cycles. Mothers are awakened less often from a state of deep sleep, which is what leads to the feeling of not getting enough sleep. Being awakened from deep sleep by a hungry, crying baby is what makes the concept of nighttime parenting unattractive and leads to exhausted mothers, fathers, and babies.

A "Hormoneous" Relationship Develops

In Chapter 1 you read that the hormone prolactin is possibly the mothering hormone and the chemical basis of God's design for the term *mother's intuition*. Three situations make prolactin increase in your body: (1) sleeping, (2) breastfeeding, and (3) touching or simply being with your baby. Sleeping with your baby allows all three of these situations to occur throughout the night. When your baby shares sleep with you, he touches you and nurses from you, which stimulates the release of more prolactin.

It is noteworthy that it is not nighttime that stimulates prolactin but the act of sleeping itself. This is why mothers are encouraged to take frequent naps and sleep with their babies during the day also.

Mothers who share sleep with their babies and have mastered this nighttime harmony often tell me that as time goes on they seem to need less sleep and feel more rested despite their babies' waking and nursing frequently during the night. Their acceptance and tolerance of nighttime mothering seem to broaden. Could this also be in God's design? Is it possible that the increased prolactin (which I also call the "perseverance hormone") could be responsible for the increase in tolerance in nighttime mothering?

There are probably many beneficial effects of sharing sleep that are in the divine design that are not known about yet. Some researchers have even suggested that mothers' and babies' sleep and dream cycles and brain wave patterns are in unison when they sleep and nurse together. Science is just beginning to confirm what God has designed and intuitive mothers have known all along—that something good happens when babies and mothers share sleep.

Breastfeeding Is Easier

When baby and mother are in close proximity they can meet each other's needs often without either one's becoming fully awake. A mother who had achieved this nighttime nursing harmony with her baby shared the following story with me: "About thirty seconds before my baby wakes for a feeding, my sleep seems to lighten and I almost wake up. [She is entering her phase of light sleep.] By being able to anticipate his feeding, I usually can start breastfeeding him just as he begins to squirm and reach for the nipple. Getting to him immediately keeps him from fully waking up, and then he drifts back into a deep sleep right after nursing."

What happens is that the baby probably nurses through the vulnerable period of awakening and then reenters the state of deep sleep. If mother and baby had not been near each other, the baby would probably have had to wake up crying to signify his need. By the time the mother reached the baby in another room, both mother and baby would have been wide awake and would have had difficulty settling back to sleep.

"My baby wants to nurse all night" is a common concern of nighttime mothering. This occasional "marathoning" also may be in accordance with God's design. Babies have periodic growth spurts during which they need extra nighttime nutrition. It is interesting that one of the oldest medical treatments for the slow weight-gaining baby is the simple advice, "Take your baby to bed and nurse."

May Be Advantageous in Child Spacing

In my experience, natural family planning in which breastfeeding is used as a contraceptive seldom works unless mothers and babies share sleep. If you believe in a divine design for child spacing, it follows that the concept of sharing sleep also may be part of God's design.

May Prevent SIDS

The current theory is that Sudden Infant Death Syndrome (SIDS) may be a basic disorder of sleep in some infants. Researchers feel that SIDS may be due to the inability of some infants to breathe automatically during the state of deep sleep or to arouse from sleep and trigger a self-start mechanism in response to a breathing problem. My hypothesis is that nursing and sharing sleep may prevent SIDS in certain high-risk infants. I have presented this hypothesis at scientific meetings in order to stimulate research in this area. Sharing sleep and nursing increase mutual sensitivity between mother and baby. This arrangement also increases the amount of REM sleep, which acts as a protective state against breathing failure. During shared sleep mother acts as a respiratory pacemaker to remind baby to breathe. (For further reading on this very sensitive topic, the reader is referred to my book *Nighttime Parenting*).

Dispelling Myths

In the following section some of the popular myths concerning sleeping with your baby will be explained and hopefully dispelled.

Myth One. "Doctor, won't she become dependent and never want to sleep alone?" Answer: yes and no. Yes, your baby will seem dependent temporarily and will not want to leave your bed. This is natural. When you are close to someone you love and you feel right about it, why give up a good thing? It's a question of trust, not dependency. Your infant trusts that you will listen to his other cues, and you trust your ability to respond appropriately to these cues.

No, your baby will not grow up to be more dependent. Your baby will eventually sleep alone; however, the age at which a child goes from oneness to separateness varies from child to child. What is important is that you allow your child to go from oneness to separateness on the terms that feel right for both of you, not according to some preconceived time chart determined by peer pressure or child-care advisers. In my experience, children who are given free access to sharing sleep actually become more secure and independent because they reach their stage of separateness when they are ready and are not hurried into separate quarters too soon.

Another consideration is that it is not the parents' responsibility to make a child independent. Parents should create an environment of security that allows the child's independence to develop naturally, rather than grudgingly.

Myth Two. "Won't we have sexual disturbances?" Nonsense! Absolutely not! This may be the bed where he was conceived. How can love between two parents adversely affect the product of their love? As a father of seven who has practiced the concept of sharing sleep, I do not think our babies have "come between us" that much.

Usually parents have the wisdom to be discreet about how much affection they show each other in front of their child at any age. A child should not come between husband and wife. The concept of the family bed and the family bedroom requires some ingenuity toward having a private place for husband and wife to be together. The master bedroom is not the only place for lovemaking to occur. Couples who have successfully enjoyed the concept of the family bed have humorously related to me that every room in the house is a potential love chamber. This attitude probably leads to more variety in the couple's sexual relations. Also it is usually not difficult, if you and your husband wish to be alone, to request kindly but firmly that your child leave your bedroom "because Mommy and Daddy want to be alone for a while." I feel it is healthy for a child to get two messages concerning the master bedroom: (1) the door is open to me if I have a strong need to be with my parents, and (2) there are private times when Mommy and Daddy want to be alone that are nonnegotiable. Again, it is the attitude within the bedroom that counts to the child, not the actual timing of physical relations.

Myth Three. "I might roll over on my baby and smother him." This is one of the oldest myths and does indeed disturb some parents; therefore, I will attempt to alleviate your fears with a thorough explanation of the subject. The biblical verse that has contributed to this myth is 1 Kings 3:19, "And this woman's son died in the night, because she lay on him." This could have been a case of sudden infant death syndrome. In early days the concept of SIDS was not fully understood and was erroneously interpreted as smothering.

Where there have been reports of babies being overlaid there has been an unusual element such as a drugged or drunk parent or too many persons squeezed into too small a space. If the account in First Kings was actually an overlaying, remember these mothers were prostitutes so conditions were far from ideal and may have involved drunkenness or crowding (1 Kings 3:16).

Safety tip! Besides one or both parents being under the influence of drugs or alcohol and overcrowding, another precaution must be mentioned. When lying on a waterbed facedown, an infant may be unable to lift his head clear of the depression that forms, or he may get his head wedged between the waterbed mattress and the bed frame. The firmer "waveless" type would be much safer or use a special covering to firm up the surface.

Mothers I have interviewed on the subject have shared with me that because infants and mothers are so physically and mentally aware of each others' presence when they sleep together, both of them would awaken immediately if overlaying did somehow occur. One mother told me that if her infant were struggling to breathe or had any signs of imminent SIDS, she would want to be by her infant's side. If her infant died by her side, she would feel that she had done everything possible to save her baby. If her infant died in another room, she would always have had the feeling she was not there when her baby needed her and that she might have been able to save his or her life.

Fathers sometimes worry about the possibility of flopping an arm over on baby or being less sensitive to baby's presence. I feel the best arrangement is for baby to be between mother and a guardrail. (See illustration on page 191.)

I make the following statements without offering any scientific documentation to support them; they stem from my pediatrician's intuition regarding sharing sleep. I feel that when a baby and a mother sleep close to each other they have a form of communication even when they are sleeping. Any disturbance in this communication network will be perceived by the mother, and she will awaken to correct the interference in these waves of communication. Experts who study SIDS no longer list overlaying as one of the causes of SIDS.

Myth Four: "Isn't this an unusual custom? What will people say?" Just the opposite is true. In most cultures from biblical times to present times (1 Kings 3:20; Luke 11:7), babies have slept with their mothers. Even in Western cultures mothers have been following this practice for years but were afraid to tell their doctors and their in-laws about it. If you want to get a feel for how prevalent this custom really is, walk into a meeting of young mothers and confide to one of them, "My baby is sleeping with me. What do you think about this arrangement?" Your confidante will probably look around to make sure nobody else is listening and then whisper back, "My baby is, too, but don't tell anybody."

These mothers are doing what their maternal instinct tells them is right, but because of erroneous cultural taboos they are made to feel that this concept may be morally wrong. Infants' sleeping with their mothers is not a recent fad but an attempt to return to traditional values that time and maternal instinct have proven to be right. Early medical books recommended the family bed. For example, a child care book written in 1840, *Management of Infancy* by A. Combe (New York: Fowlers and Wells), stated that "there can scarcely be a doubt that at least during the first four weeks and during winter and early spring a child will thrive better if allowed to sleep beside its mother's side and be cherished by her warmth than if placed in a separate bed." An East African tribal chief once said, "At night when there was no sun to warm me, my mother's arms and her body took its place."

I predict that the family bed will be practiced more and more until it becomes the usual custom in Western culture. This sleeping arrangement will mature in popularity as will many of the more traditional and time-proven concepts of child care. It is interesting that breastfeeding was unusual in the 1950s in the Western culture. Now many of these "unusual" customs are coming back because, in reality, they never left the intuitive hearts of mothers.

Myth Five. "But my doctor told me not to let our baby sleep in our bed." Parents shouldn't ask their doctors about sleep sharing, and doctors shouldn't give definite yes or no answers. This doctor's response is a carryover from the "dependency pediatrics" of the fifties and sixties when a mother's intuition had been so culturally programmed out that a new mother felt more comfortable taking her doctor's advice than following her own God-given instinct. The doctor was put on the spot to come up with a rather dogmatic answer on a subject for which he had no training. Most doctors elected to join the camp of "separate sleepers" because the detachment and separation philosophy was popular at that time and there was some security in numbers.

There are some aspects of child care on which your doctor does not need to give you advice. Where your baby sleeps and whether or not you should let your baby cry in a particular situation can be answered only by you. When it comes to maternal-infant attachment (see Chapter 1), you should follow your intuition above the advice of anyone else since the other person has no biological attachment to your infant.

Take heart. Some doctors realize they will have to spend less time correcting sleep problems in children at a later age if they counsel parents on how to prevent sleep problems in their children at an early age. Fortunately, female doctors and the wives of male doctors are influencing the medical profession to promote God-given maternal instincts concerning sleeping arrangements.

Father Feelings About Sharing Sleep

"I want my baby to sleep next to me, but my husband refuses." It is vital to God's order for the family that both husband and wife agree on where the baby sleeps. If this is a problem in your family, let me offer the following advice. Many husbands fall prey to the previously discussed myths. Read this chapter together; listen to the cassette tape *Surviving Your Baby's Sleep Patterns* (for publication information, see the end of Chapter 9). Pray together asking God to guide you on the best sleeping arrangements for your family. Discuss the advantages of sharing sleep. If God's design for the family is followed, your child should never be allowed to divide you as a couple. This statement may not sit well with some parenting organizations, but I have given this concept of God's order for the family considerable thought and prayer. I have seen disastrous consequences to the whole family result from the "overattachment syndrome" (see Chapter 1).

Father, if you have ambivalent feelings about your baby's sleeping in your bed, I urge you to trust your wife's instinct. This is one instance in which mother knows best. Having the baby sleep between parents concerns some fathers. If this bothers you, let me suggest the sleeping arrangement shown in the illustration above; baby can sleep between mother and a guardrail if you prefer.

Actually, once reluctant fathers get used to sleep sharing, most of them learn to enjoy it. It is an occasion for wonderful closeness that many fathers initially accept and later enjoy. If you consider how little time you spend being physically close to your baby during the day, then nighttime fathering may be a boost to your father-infant relationship. Again, whatever sleeping arrangement gets all three the most quality sleep is the right sleeping arrangement for your family. King-size beds are a wise investment for all new families and are actually cheaper than buying a lot of unnecessary baby furniture that your baby will probably not use or outgrow quickly.

Be prepared for a few humorous situations such as the one we experienced when our baby daughter got her directions mixed up and rolled over to nurse from me instead of Martha. You might also enjoy the experience one father related to me. When he awakes because of some worry, instead of letting his worry keep him from going back to sleep, he looks over and sees the face of his child sleeping soundly within the security of those who love him. The sight of a peaceful child usually will dispel any worry of the world since it keeps his priorities in perspective.

Are There Any Disadvantages to the Family Bed?

Occasionally parents complain that they cannot sleep well with their baby in their bed. There are several explanations for this.

When parents have not welcomed their baby into their bed early enough, neither parents nor baby is used to the arrangement. Most squirmers can be taught to respect other sleeping family members' space by being picked up and put into another room or sleeping location. They soon get the idea that squirming is an unacceptable nocturnal habit.

Parents may try the family bed reluctantly. They may accept their baby into their bed out of desperation: "I'll try any arrangement so we can get some sleep, but I really don't like this idea." A baby senses when he is an unwelcome guest in the family bed. These negative vibrations turn a positive experience into a negative one that seldom works.

Occasionally, a Christian mother who sincerely loves her children will share with me, "I've been with my children all day long; I simply do not want my baby in my bed. This is my special time with my husband alone." This feeling should be respected, and I fully sympathize with this mother's wish.

Most children wean themselves from the family bed by two to three years of age and into their own rooms by three to four years of age. Thereafter they sleep comfortably and independently, returning to the comfort of the parents' bed only during particularly stressful times. Weaning from the parents' bed usually requires intermediate steps, such as a mattress next to your bed for a while or the alternative arrangement of sleeping with an older sibling.

I am absolutely certain that there are no psychosexual disturbances that are caused by sleep sharing. In my opinion, this is God's design for sleeping for most families, but you must be comfortable with it to work for you. If you are having sleep problems within your family, ask God for guidance concerning the right sleeping arrangement.

A discussion of common sleep problems and their solutions follows in the next chapter.

CHAPTER 9

COMMON
SLEEP
PROBLEMS

At the beginning of the previous chapter I mentioned that children have different sleep cycles from those of adults. They are aroused from sleep more easily and have more difficulty resettling. Nighttime is scary for little people who are used to being with or seeing somebody. The following are the most common reasons for children awakening:

1. Physical discomfort—teething, hunger, wet diaper, stuffy nose, ear infection, pin worms, uncomfortable sleeping position, gas pains and stomachaches, allergies, kidney infection.
2. Noises—a squeaky crib, environmental noises (barking dog, cars, weather).
3. Emotional disturbances—nightmares, dreams, fears, or separation anxieties.

Some common sleep problems occur at various ages. These usually fall into one of two classes: (1) child not going to sleep, and (2) child not staying asleep.

Remember, difficult problems do not have easy solutions. Sleep problems are among the most individual problems in pediatrics. The following proposed solutions may or may not fit your individual baby.

Situation One. "My baby is six weeks old. She used to awaken only once or twice and then resettle after nursing. Now she awakens every two hours for a feeding, and I have difficulty resettling her. I'm exhausted." Perhaps your baby is going through a growth spurt and needs to marathon nurse. Redefining your daytime priorities is necessary during this temporary marathoning in order for you to catnap during the day and recharge your nocturnal parenting battery at night. Marathon nursing is one instance when it would be wise to welcome your baby into your bed and enjoy nursing there. This relationship will give her more milk during this growth spurt and should interrupt your sleep less.

Situation Two. "My baby is six months old and waking more often and resettling less well, yet he doesn't seem hungry." At about six months of age, babies are awakened by physical discomforts such as teething, stuffy nose, and the collection of profuse saliva in the back of the throat that usually accompanies teething. Babies begin teething pain between four to six months, and if this pain occurs during the light phase of sleep, they may awaken. The increased mucous produced during teething may lodge in your baby's throat and awaken him. Hunger is also a possibility, but hungry babies usually settle well once fed. The mother should try a long nursing before she goes to bed and then make sure the baby really feeds when he wakes up at night, rather than having a series of wakings in which he sucks just long enough to lull himself back to sleep but does not deal with his hunger. You may have to actually sit up in bed and pick the baby up so he will actively feed long enough to get a full tummy.

Six-month-old babies often do not resettle easily for two reasons. First, they are intensely interested in their environment and want to look around. For this reason, try to keep the lights off and use quiet, soothing words. Second, not seeing the mother he feels and touches all day long may also keep baby from resettling. Remember that your six- to nine-month-old baby might be suffering separation anxiety because he lacks object permanency, a capacity your baby will develop toward the end of his second year.

Situation Three. "My baby is one and a half years old and awakens happily at 4:00 A.M. ready to get up and play, but I am not." The baby needs some repatterning similar to the baby who won't go to bed. It is unrealistic to put some babies down at 6:00 to 7:00 P.M. and expect them to sleep until 7:00 A.M. Repattern your baby's sleep by delaying her nap until later in the afternoon, keeping her up later in the evening, and mothering or fathering her to bed later. Many mothers confess, "She's not ready for bed at 7:00, but I'm ready for her to go to bed." Realistically, I feel children who are put to bed early miss some meaningful evening time with their fathers.

If repatterning is necessary, the eighteen-month-old to two-year-old child is verbal enough to understand that nighttime is not playtime. Give your child a loving hug, then tell her firmly that Mommy and Daddy are going back to bed and you expect her to do the same. The baby who wakes up for playtime but does not seem to be afraid can be made to understand your policy regarding playtime and sleeptime. You may offer to lie down with your child or let her lie on a mattress next to your bed, or you can convey in some other way that this is not playtime.

Some parents feel they should not have to negotiate or use creative ways to get their children to sleep. They feel it is in their power as authority figures to say when and where the child sleeps. I continually affirm the necessity for a strong authority role for parents, but authority does not mean your mind is closed to what your child is telling you.

Wise authority stems from two-way communication in which you are in charge and reserve the right to make the final decision, but you are still open to listen to your child's cues. Your child should sense your openness. Many parents get hung up by the term *manipulation* and feel that if a child does not sleep at preassigned hours in a preassigned place, then any other alternative the child wishes is manipulation. This is simply not true. I'm horrified by advice that says if a child won't stay in her crib, put a net over her crib so she can't get out. If a child is continuously standing up in her crib, rattling her cage, or climbing out, the message is clear—she doesn't want to sleep in her crib. The parent can insist that she will sleep in the crib, but this leads to unending nighttime struggles in which nobody wins. The wise parent may listen to what the child is actually saying and give the child other alternatives of sleeping arrangements. In my opinion, this is not manipulation. This is communication; this is trust. It is trusting your child that she really should have a say about where she feels right sleeping; it is trusting yourself that you are confidently and appropriately responding to your child's cues.

Situation Four. "My two-year-old is awakening more and more frequently and generally will not stay in his crib. Sometimes when I get up in the morning I find him asleep outside our bedroom door. He's becoming increasingly more difficult to resettle in the middle of the night unless I stay with him." This child is exhibiting separation anxiety and probably has nightmares. By two years of age most infants have achieved object permanency and can understand that Mother is in another room. Yet, the child who falls asleep outside the parents' door obviously wants to sleep in the parents' room. Is it too humiliating to parents to listen to their children? Welcome your child into your bedroom, and if his sleeping with you is not an option with which you feel right, give your child a mattress or a sleeping bag next to your bed. At this point you can tell him firmly that if he wishes to sleep in the family bedroom, you expect him to sleep quietly until the morning and not disturb you. Tell him, "If you wake up, you know we're right here and you can go back to sleep."

Most of the time, in return for sleeping in the family bedroom, your two year old will keep quiet so he can continue this sleeping arrangement. Being allowed into the family bed or the family bedroom is a real boost to the child's self-esteem. You are conveying to your child the message that he is as important to you during the night as he is during the day.

Situation Five. "My two year old just doesn't know when to give up. I know she's tired by her droopy eyelids and her yawning, but she fights going to bed." Some children do not want to put away the excitement of the daytime world. In this case, you should know best, and oftentimes a child is waiting for someone in authority to override her lack of wisdom.

Have a quiet hour before a realistic bedtime; instead of energetic activities, try wind-down activities such as reading a soothing story and rocking in a rocking chair. Bedtime rituals are good. A warm bath, a story, and a good-night lullaby make a winning combination to help heavy eyelids overcome busy minds. Fathers should assume the major role in the bedtime ritual.

Situation Six. "It takes my husband too long to put our two year old to bed. We have a large family, and we run out of time." This is a common ploy of young children in a large family. Sometimes the only time a child gets one-on-one attention from Dad is at bedtime, and he is going to play this special time for all he can get. Parents need to accept this as a normal attachment phase, and be thankful that their children want to be with them. Do the best you can. One of the realistic expectations of fathering a large family is that he can't give enough time to all his children all the time. I feel that your children and your God will understand this dilemma.

Situation Seven. "My three year old is afraid to go to bed alone and wakes frequently with scary nightmares." Children from two to three years of age have vivid imaginations and often distort reality in their dreams; a dog may look like a dinosaur in a dream. Attempt to find out what the scary thing is. It may be something your child saw on TV that day. Make a game out of the situation by saying, "Daddy went into your room and chased out the dragon." This may work well, but I am a little leery of always fighting fantasy with fantasy. Some children may see through this or may think there really are dragons in their rooms. Game playing to alleviate fears and chase out scary animals at least conveys to your child your sympathy and your availability to help. Often children need a parent's continued presence for the "dragon" to be gone.

Situation Eight. "My six-month-old baby wants to nurse at night." The case of the frequent night nurser is one of the most common and most exhausting occupational hazards of nocturnal parenting. Because I'm reluctant to offer advice that might deprive some babies of a basic need, I will attempt to explain why some infants nurse at night and why you should *not* discourage it. I feel that it is God's design for some infants to nurse more at night, and I do not wish to be listed in the Lord's "Book of False Prophets" for bad baby advice, for which some day I may be held accountable.

Babies want or need to breastfeed during the night because they are easily distracted during daytime nursing. Between two and three months many babies become interested in the sensual world around them. They suck a little and look a little, constantly interrupting their feeding because something more interesting comes along. During the day there is often more competition for the baby's and the mother's interest. However, at night the baby has the mother all to himself so that there are fewer distractions for both of them. These nocturnal nuisances are especially common in busy households or in those with breastfeeding mothers who work outside the home during the day. Remember, babies are perfect parasites, and I feel God designed them that way.

Babies learn at a very early age how to get what they need. Some child psychologists would consider night nursing a manipulative behavior, a way of getting what a baby wants—not what he or she needs. In my opinion, most babies nurse at night from need rather than habit.

Situation Nine. "My five-month-old daughter cannot sleep longer than an hour at night, even though she sleeps in our bed. When she wakes she screams or fights and insists on staying awake. Then when she goes back to sleep she tosses and turns. And she can't nap unless I lie down with her the whole time."

Allergies (environmental or dietary) can greatly disturb sleep. The baby may be showing no other signs of allergy, or the fitful sleep may also be accompanied by rashes, colic (or history of colic), fussiness, chronic ear infections, and/or persistent runny nose and puffy, reddened eyes. The profile of this type of night waking includes fitful tossing and turning, crying out, waking every sixty to ninety minutes, crib rocking or head bumping. Often this baby cannot nap for longer than twenty minutes and the mother is exhausted.

Cow's milk proteins in the mother's diet (or directly in the baby's diet if on formula or eating dairy products) is often the culprit. Bovine beta-lactoglobulin has been shown to enter human milk, causing a sensitive baby to have sleep problems. Other protein foods, such as wheat, corn or other grains, certain nuts, shellfish, or egg whites may also be implicated. If she is breastfeeding, the mother must eliminate the offending food from her diet and also from her baby's diet. Start with cow's milk and all cow's milk products (even reading labels to detect whey or casein). Improvement is usually seen within one or two days, although often the symptoms will reappear temporarily around the fifth or sixth day. The food should be eliminated for at least three to four weeks. There may be several offending foods that need to be eliminated simultaneously and then gradually reintroduced on a rotation basis.

Testing for food allergy can be very uncertain and most of the determination will be on a trial and error basis. Consulting a nutritionist or food allergist may be necessary if the mother becomes confused or feels she needs help pinpointing the problem foods. (*Tracking Down Hidden Food Allergies,* by William Crook, M.D., is a helpful book.) She may also need a calcium supplement to be sure she gets the required daily food allowance (RDA) of 1500 mg for a lactating woman. Environmental irritants such as smoke, feather pillows, molds, mildew, certain laundry products, polyester sleepwear, and even some bedroom furniture made with particleboard can be responsible.

Situation Ten. "I have a two-month-old baby whose colic is not getting better and who spits up a lot after feedings. The worst part, though, is the way she wakes with painful cries at night. She seems okay as soon as I nurse her, and she goes back to sleep well, but then the whole thing starts all over again. We have tried everything, and there is no relief."

A newly recognized cause of night waking is the Pediatric Regurgitation Syndrome. The acidic stomach juices are regurgitating up into the esophagus causing a painful, burning sensation. This syndrome usually includes frequent spitting up and a baby who cries a lot and awakens frequently. Breastfeeding upon night waking relieves the pain momentarily. Occasionally, babies with this syndrome do not actually spit up so that the regurgitation is not observed, and the diagnosis may be missed. Special abdominal X rays confirm the diagnosis, and treatment is with medications.

Let me share a humorous story that happened when one of our children was enjoying one of her many middle-of-the-night meals. I am a very light sleeper and am easily awakened by unusual sounds. Our rather large Labrador retriever has a habit of drinking out of her water bowl on the back porch with an exceptionally loud slurp. One night this sound occurred, and I jumped out of bed determined to put an end to our dog's nighttime thirst quenching. My wife was quick to inform me that it was not our dog I heard but our baby who was nursing vigorously because she had been particularly distracted from nursing that day. I feel that God has given us all a sense of humor in order that we may survive parenting and our children may survive their parents.

A Summary of Bedtime Suggestions

1. *Consider the concept of sharing sleep.* Sleeping with or close to the parents will prevent or alleviate most sleeping problems in children.

2. *Have a quiet time before going to bed, a time of winding down.*

3. *Parent your child to sleep; don't just put your child to sleep.* A breast (or bottle) and a rocking chair make a winning combination for the tiny infant. Mothers, lie down in bed with your infant, allowing him to fall asleep in your arms and at your breasts. Some babies have to be rocked to sleep before being put down; others like to be put down awake and then mothered or fathered to sleep in your bed and your arms (you may fall asleep before your child does). Encourage the child's favorite bedtime ritual if it is a wind-down not a windup activity.

4. *Engage in "back to the womb" activities.*

a. Give your baby a before-bedtime bath and a soothing massage.

b. Make sure your baby is covered suitably. Some babies settle better in less coverings that allow them more freedom of movement, but others settle better when they are securely swaddled.

c. Lie down with your baby and snuggle, cradling your baby in your arms. My wife calls this ritual "nestle nursing." This continuum from a warm bath to warm arms to warm breasts to a warm bed will usually induce sleep.

d. Use a moving bed such as a cradle or a rocking bed. Rocking in general, whether in your arms or in a cradle, should be about seventy beats per minute, which is the rhythm of the heartbeat your baby has grown accustomed to.

e. Immediately after putting your baby down to sleep, to avoid protests of succumbing to sleep, lay your hands on your baby's back or head and rhythmically pat his or her back or bottom. Very gradually lessen the pressure of the pats as you notice your baby drift off to sleep.

f. Adjust baby's sleeping positions. In their first few weeks, tiny infants sleep best on their side. Place a rolled up towel in the crevice between baby's back and the mattress. The safest position, however, is putting baby to sleep on his back. As discussed on pages 158–59, back-sleeping helps reduce the risk of SIDS.

g. Play a soothing tape recording of running water or ocean sounds, classical music, a metronome or a clock.

h. Provide a warm fuzzy. Falling asleep on Dad's chest is a warm fuzzy. Tiny babies enjoy this sleeping arrangement when they are small enough not to wiggle off easily, usually during their first two months. A lambskin mat is also a warm fuzzy that babies can get used to and that will condition them to sleep wherever the mat is placed.

5. *Soundproof the sleeping area.* Oil all the squeaks in the crib and put rubber coasters under the crib posts or a rug under the crib.

6. *Run a humidifier in the bedroom,* especially during the dry winter months of central heating.

7. *Be sure all systems are clear*—clear nose, dry diaper, full tummy.

8. *Pray soothing and reassuring prayers* that convey to the child that Jesus will watch over him or her during the night. Sensing the presence of God watching over him or her is comforting to the child who feels that nighttime is a scary, lonely time. Avoid the common scary prayer of "If I die, I pray the Lord my soul to keep." No child should be put to bed with the suggestion that he or she might not wake up.

For more detailed suggestions on getting your baby to sleep, see the reference list at the end of this chapter.

The psychological rationale for allowing babies to cry themselves to sleep is reinforcement: negative behavior if reinforced will continue and if not reinforced will not continue. It sounds nice if parents think that crying is negative behavior, but in many cases this is not true. Crying is baby's language to communicate a need. If a baby's language is responded to during the day but not during the night, the baby may be confused and may experience a feeling of "not rightness" that goes against the goals of parenting mentioned throughout this book. "But," you say, "Doctor, this waking up could be a habit, not a need." Yes, I agree. Habits are negotiable; needs are not. If your baby's cries are reaching increasing intensity and your inner parenting voice says this is a need you must satisfy, then listen to yourself first and not a book or an adviser. If your baby's individual cries wind down shortly after they begin and your inner parenting sensor is not heavily signaled, then this is probably a habit. Habits are easily broken; needs are not.

The Exhausted-Mother Syndrome

You may gather from this discussion that I favor nighttime parenting. I do. It's part of the investment in your child's trust relationship with his caregiver and his emerging sense of feeling right and of self-esteem. However, mothers may reach a point where their maternal reserves run out and negative feelings toward their children set in. When giving of herself at night compromises her effectiveness as a mother during the day, the entire mother-child relationship suffers a net loss. Her marriage may be strained too. If you are a mother who has reached this point, your need for sleep takes priority over your child's needs for nocturnal parenting. This is a difficult decision. Sometimes I step out on a limb and advise a tired, exhausted mother that for the benefit of the entire family, her need to sleep must come first. I also preface my advice by stating: "This is a problem in which you are not going to like any of the solutions, but you must try something in order to recharge your mothering reserves."

Survival Tips

Shift work. For a couple of nights the father gets up with the baby, rocks the baby, walks with the baby, gives a bottle if bottle fed, and if nothing else works, takes the baby for a car ride. Meanwhile, the mother sleeps (or tries to). If she is breastfeeding and the baby is not settled after feeding, and hunger is not the obvious cause, then the father should rock, walk, or burp the baby while the mother goes back to sleep. Certainly if the mother has a job outside the home during the day, both parents should share these nocturnal interruptions.

Sedatives. This solution is unpopular, but it is certainly worth a try when you have reached the end of your rope. Sedatives, if used for only a few nights, will not harm your baby or be addicting (long-range usage is addicting and sedative-induced sleep is usually not the highest quality sleep). Ask your doctor for a sedative for your baby to be used for two or three nights in order to reset his sleep cycles and allow you to recharge your battery. You may need to try several different sedatives in varying dosages before you find one that works. Again, I recommend this only after you have tried everything else and have reached the honest decision that your need for sleep takes precedence over your baby's need for nocturnal parenting.

Letters from Tired Parents

Because sleep problems are one of the greatest occupational hazards of early parenting, I want to share some letters from mothers who have written to me concerning various sleeping arrangements for various family situations. I hope you are able to identify with some of these mothers and profit from their advice.

Dear Dr. Sears,

After the birth of my first baby I went through an experience that I was in no way prepared for: postpartum depression. The tension and stress I felt from suddenly becoming a new mother caused me to actually be scared of my baby at times. Compounding my tensions was the thought that since I'd be returning to work soon I felt like I would be "abandoning" my baby. All of these doubts and uncertainties were manifested in a bout of insomnia that stretched for four days.

I'd lay my baby in her crib at night, then go to my room and just pray that I would get some sleep before she woke up for her next feeding. This was a bad mistake. While I tried to force myself to relax I was aware of every turn, gurgle, and sigh that she was making in the next room. [Mother and baby were not in harmony.]

By the time I called my pediatrician I was desperate for help. He suggested that I bring her into bed with me at night. I tried it, and although I was slightly nervous at first, afraid I would roll onto her, I quickly found that I was able to sleep and relax when she was next to me. I also think that having a family bed has brought us closer together as mother and daughter. [They are now in harmony.] Spending the night together, holding her and then breastfeeding her when she wakes up has made me feel less uncomfortable about leaving her with a sitter during the day. Besides, like my husband says, what better way to start a day than to wake up with your lover and your child next to you.

Dear Dr. Sears,

There were many reasons why we decided to have our baby sleep with us. Although there were some problems, we have been able to overcome them. My husband was afraid that he would roll over on her, but he never did. Friends told me that the romance would go out of our marriage if we had a baby sleep with us. If anything, I think it has made us more loving. We know she is safe and she has us there if she needs us.

We did run out of room as she got older. That problem was solved by attaching a one-sided crib to our bed. We removed one side of a crib and adjusted the mattress to the level of our mattress. Now she loves to go to her "bed" and get tucked in. She can still see us and crawl to us if she needs to. Having her with us has made nursing a breeze.

She almost never cries at night or, for that matter, during the day. She and her father are very close. Occasionally she still will fall asleep on his stomach. All in all, having her with us has been great. We feel good knowing she is secure and not lonely. More importantly, she knows we are there for her if she needs us. We will miss her when she goes to her own bed.

The following letter illustrates how a couple incorporated their nighttime parenting into their general style of attachment parenting.

Dear Dr. Sears,

After meeting our six-month-old son, his grandfather was impressed that John seemed so secure and well-adjusted. This was an encouragement that our parenting principles are on the right track.

Our pregnancy was entirely positive, with my husband participating in every way possible. Childbirth classes were taken seriously . . . homework included. A number of people had "prepared" us for the "terrible" experience labor was to be; consequently we were happily surprised to have a very positive birth. As a couple, those hours during labor and birth brought us the closest we had ever been, and I felt I was literally watching the two of us become a family.

Our baby roomed-in with me in the hospital, creating a special three-day private family time for us. The first weeks of parenting did not bring the tension between us that we had been warned about. This baby was someone we both had planned for and wanted very much, and we were ready to pour ourselves into the little life.

Totally breastfeeding and nursing our son on demand encouraged us to try the family bed; a big plus is not getting out of a warm bed several times a night to feed the baby, and we have fine-tuned our nursing techniques so that now neither Mom nor baby fully wakes for a feeding.

My husband was to be the barometer in this relationship. Wanting to respect his feelings, we decided that if he thought it was not working out, we would get a crib. We don't have one yet. All three of us enjoy the closeness, and we rest secure knowing John is OK—warm, right next to us, and easy to find in the dark. In anticipation of a large family, we are making plans for a larger bed. John rarely wakes up crying in the morning. He is content and happy, a nice way to start each day.

On particularly demanding days, I appreciate nursing, knowing that if John were bottle fed, I would tend to bottle propping. This way I must sit down and spend some time touching and holding him. I cannot compromise my responsibilities.

We travel together almost everywhere. As a twosome my husband and I were very devoted, and bringing our son with us now is the natural extension of our loyalty. We find we like to be together and have not as yet wished for the proverbial weekend away.

My husband and I feel very positive about the way we parent, and we work hard at being a couple as well.

Unfortunately, people's opinions and comments do matter. We dislike hiding the fact that we sleep together or nurse on demand in order to avoid judgment. We view all the advice given us as unfortunate and negative. It does not sit well with us; we do not see any error in our ways, and we do not run out to engage a baby-sitter. Deep inside we "know" to continue as before, but closer to the surface I panic. (Are women affected more by others' opinions than men?)

When someone suggests that "we must let our baby know where he stands" and "make certain he is not running our lives," it leads to self-doubt. Until it is brought to my attention, it doesn't even occur to me that I may be taken advantage of. If I don't feel right about leaving him in certain situations and he doesn't like to be left, are we both wrong? If I leave him at someone else's recommendation and we're both miserable, who benefits?

Ultimately, I know that the wisdom that we parents need must come from the Lord. Though people may err in offering damaging advice, I, too, err in putting so much stake in their words. Perhaps God allows this to teach me to trust Him, and to underscore the importance of having His Word dwell richly in my heart. As I continue to grow in Him, my confidence will be increasingly in Him, and when questions arise regarding parenting, I'll know who to ask.

This chapter has barely skimmed the surface of what is a very difficult problem in parenting. For this reason, the following references are recommended to parents who are struggling to develop a style of night-time parenting:

Surviving Your Baby's Sleep Patterns by William Sears, M.D. (Ventura, California: Vision House, 1984). This hour-and-a-half cassette tape contains many testimonies from tired parents in my practice who have also used the power of prayer to make it through the night. This tape is available from Vision House, 2300 Knoll Drive, Ventura, California, 93003.

The Family Bed by Thevenin Tine. This two-hundred-page book presents the author's experience and study of the advantages of sleeping with your baby. It is available from the author at P.O. Box 16004, Minneapolis, Minnesota, 55416.

Nighttime Parenting—How to Get Your Baby and Child to Sleep by William Sears, M.D. (New York: New American Library, 1987).

CHAPTER 10

THE DILEMMA OF THE WORKING MOTHER

One day on a TV show, my wife, Martha, and I were discussing my first book, *Creative Parenting*, with the host. I was asked my views on the working mother. As I was struggling to muster up some inoffensive answer, Martha put a touch of reality in the show by proclaiming, "If I hadn't been a working mother while my husband was a student, he wouldn't be here today as a physician and author even to answer this question." Women have a way of getting right to the point when commenting on the subjects that are written about by men but experienced only by women. This was, however, in our early years as parents and, even though Martha worked part-time only enough to pay the rent, we now realize we could have made better choices.

The issue is not the working mother. Mothers have always "worked" and worked very hard. The issue is working at a job outside the home. Like so many issues in parenting, difficult problems do not have easy solutions.

Choices

Many sincere, caring, and devout Christian mothers are faced with the dilemma of having both to mother and to work outside the home. For this reason, I wrote this section with much prayer and consultation so that my comments would offer understanding support and advice, not judgment.

Many of you have already made the choice between returning to work and staying at home, but if you are having difficulty with this important decision, here are some important considerations that, if supported by prayer and counsel, will help you.

How Does Being a Full-Time Mother Affect the Child?

It has been stated previously that a strong mother-infant attachment is God's design so the young can reach their fullest potential. The development of this attachment is an ongoing maturing process that begins with the mother's strong biological commitment to her baby. Just being close to each other allows her God-given instinct, or mother's intuition, to develop to its fullest potential and gives her baby the environment of love and security to help him or her develop to his or her fullest potential.

The harmonious relationship. Being constantly in touch and in tune with her baby allows both mother and infant to be in harmony with each other. Mother, your baby has a need and gives you a cue. You pick up on this cue and appropriately respond to the need. When this happens, your baby is motivated to continue giving cues because he trusts your consistent and appropriate response. You become more comfortable with your responses because you see the feedback and appreciation from your baby. The end result of the harmonious relationship is that you accomplish two of your three parenting goals: (1) you know your child and (2) your child feels right. This feeling of mutual rightness within mother and child results in your child's acting right; a child who feels right and acts right is more of a joy to parent. The mother who senses this positive feedback from her baby feels right mothering, and the entire mother-child relationship is elevated to a higher level. A strong mother-infant attachment is especially important for the high-need child (see Chapter 4) and has far-reaching effects on later childhood.

The "hormoneous" relationship. In Chapter 1, the hormone prolactin, the milk-producing hormone, was postulated to be the chemical basis for mother's intuition. Just being close to your baby is a powerful stimulus for prolactin secretion, which further stimulates the mothering instinct, and the cycle goes on. What a beautiful design! Science is finally proving God's design that both mother and child benefit from being close to each other.

These concepts of a harmonious and a "hormoneous" relationship are particularly meaningful for the new mother who previously had a high-recognition job and worried about whether she would be able to be fulfilled by full-time mothering. Let me advise this mother to practice as early as possible all the disciplines in the attachment style of parenting. More often than not I notice that mothers who really practice these disciplines from the time of the child's birth usually elect not to return to work. One mother who found this attachment feeling shared with me: "Because I really liked my job, I had planned to return to work when my baby was three months old. Now, I can't return to work; I'm addicted to her. I never knew there could be so much joy in being a mother. My friends can't understand how I can stay home all day with my baby, but I love it." The term *addiction* is a good one for this feeling of attachment when this relationship is allowed to develop according to God's design.

What Are the Effects of Mother-Infant Separation

Essentially, both mother and baby are deprived of the benefits of mother-baby attachment. An important part of the mother-infant attachment design, which a mother deciding to return to work should evaluate, is that in order for a baby to grow and develop to his or her fullest potential, the baby must first learn a consistent attachment. He must learn this before he or she can comfortably handle separation. Child development experts believe that a child should separate from the mother on his or her own terms in order to explore his world, but the mother should not separate from the baby. Separation from the baby during the sensitive period from six to eighteen months may deprive the baby of the person who gives him or her the security to attempt independent tasks. As a result, the baby may regress in his or her developmental skills.

To what degree this level of attachment is weakened depends on (1) the need level of the baby, (2) how separation-sensitive the baby is, (3) the substitute caregiver's ability to respond appropriately to the baby's needs, (4) how much you are away from your baby, and (5) to a lesser degree, what the mother does when she is with her baby. I feel the main effect of prolonged mother-infant separation is that the baby may become confused and insecure.

Early in the mother-infant communication process the baby learns to expect a certain response to certain cues. He or she learns that his or her needs will be consistently and appropriately met and that his or her cues will be consistently understood; this is called "imprinting," or attaching one's self to one's primary caregiver. Substitute caregivers, no matter how caring, how loving, and how Christian, do not have this God-given biological attachment to your baby. They do not enjoy the previously mentioned harmonious and "hormoneous" relationship. When an infant's cues are not consistently and appropriately met, he or she stops cueing. His trust in his or her care-giving environment is weakened.

The feedback a baby receives for a developmental accomplishment is one of the most stimulating factors toward his or her development. For example, the way a mother responds to a child's primitive attempt to communicate verbally is a powerful stimulator toward a child's speech development. An infant who does not receive his or her anticipated reward becomes less motivated.

How About Quality Time?

Quality time is an example of New Age thinking (everyone going for his or her own potential) and has been capitalized upon by the child-care industry. This concept has become popular because it alleviates the guilt a mother sometimes feels when she returns to a full-time job outside the home while her baby is very young.

Actually, the idea of quality time developed in reference to fathers working long hours, often far away from home. They had little time to be with their children, but it was considered "quality time." This rationale has now been taken up by working mothers. The child who now receives quality time from both parents is squeezed in between their busy careers at their convenience.

This quality-time concept ignores some basic truths: children are spontaneous; their learning is often mood dependent; and they have unanticipated needs. Although God made children resilient and adaptable, their needs cannot be scheduled. One of the fallacies of child care is the feeling that parents always have to be stimulating or giving input to their children. The parent as a constant giver is only part of the parenting role. Many times the major role is simply being available and approachable when teachable moments occur.

This quality-time concept allows many couples to justify their lifestyles. Why is only the parent-child unit blessed with quality time? Why can't school teachers dismiss their students after only one hour of quality-time teaching instead of a full day of quantity time? Why not say to your boss, "I am only going to work an hour today, but it will be quality time"? This new math for parents says one hour of quality time equals seven hours of quantity time.

In some situations, such as that of a single working mother, quality time is really the best that can be accomplished. One sincere, caring Christian mother shared with me: "I have to work all day; so quality time is all I can afford. I give up a lot of time I would ordinarily spend on entertainment to be with my child, so that when I'm not working I'm fully devoted to my child. Besides quality time, I probably give him more quantity time than many nonworking mothers who spend a lot of time each day pursuing their own forms of entertainment." This mother is truly doing the best she can do.

Is There an Answer?

Beware of the cycle of nonattachment, which is a subtle problem that creeps into the lives of some mothers and babies. A mother who has a priority outside the home or who lacks confidence in her mothering abilities may have difficulty really getting into mothering and forming a close mother-infant attachment. Although this mother sincerely loves her child, she has ambivalent feelings about attachment mothering and resorts to an increasing use of substitute caregivers. Since the mother is not confident in responding to the baby's cues, she does not do so appropriately. As a result of this loss of appropriate feedback from his or her mother, the infant does not reward her with his or her own feedback of appreciation that would, in turn, stimulate her mothering. Mother and baby gradually drift further apart, the mother into her career outside the home and the baby into dependence on the substitute caregiver. Periodic attempts to get back into mothering are uncomfortable and therefore unsuccessful because the continuum of mother-infant attachment has been interrupted at a very early stage. The cycle of nonattachment is a particular problem when there is a mismatch of temperaments between mother and baby.

Often there are no easily identifiable effects of detachment on the older child. However, studies have shown that daughters of career-outside-the-home mothers do tend to place more emphasis on non-mothering careers, and the cycle continues into the

221

next generation. God's design for infant attachment continues to be weakened.

"I want to work for my own fulfillment."

"I want to use my education."

"If I stayed home all day, I would go stir crazy."

"I am a better mother if I am away from my child for a while and also am fulfilled outside the home."

These are real feelings from real Christian mothers who truly love their children. Again, understanding the dilemma of today's women is more important than being judgmental. It helps to remember that developing a harmonious mother-infant attachment is the main issue, not whether a mother has to stay at home. While full-time mothering definitely gives this harmony a more stable foundation, there is more to be considered.

To understand better the dilemma of the working mother, review what has happened historically to the changing roles of women. In past generations, even in biblical times, women worked at home. Proverbs 31:10–31 is a beautiful description of the working mother at home. However—and this is an important consideration—the father also usually worked at home. The family business operated out of the home or farm. Parenting and working were integrated. With the coming of industrialization and urbanization, men began leaving the home to work. Men became more educated and prepared to join the workforce, and women were culturally prepared for motherhood at home. In the first half of the twentieth century two world wars took women out of their homes into the industrial world to do traditionally "male" jobs. Next, the educational system equally prepared boys and girls to "become something," and for women, this "something" was not motherhood.

Today's women are given many more options, many more career choices. If you ask a class of high school girls what they are going to be, seldom will you get the response of "I'm going to be a homemaker" or "wife and mother." Although no one actually has said it, the subtle message is that full-time mothering is less fulfilling and has a lower status than a job outside the home. Women have begun leaving home just as men did in previous generations. Day care is the parent. "Get out and work; get fulfilled" is the message which fits in nicely with the secular ideas that gained prominence in the sixties. Total fulfillment at all cost, fulfillment from without and not from within, has become the goal of the times.

As a result of this philosophy, many women have come to feel more fulfilled by careers outside the home than by motherhood. I have counseled many women who believe they wouldn't feel right if they stayed home full time and cared for their children. They would do so resentfully; their children would sense the underlying tensions; and both they and their children would lose. But, by pursuing a part-time career outside the home or, *best of all, inside the home,* a mother can have her self-image—not selfish image as some people would say—elevated; she feels better as a person and therefore feels better as a mother. Both mother and children profit. I support the mother who has come to this decision after much prayer and deliberation.

If you have these ambivalent feelings concerning the dual-career dilemma, the following suggestions may help you to resolve them. (1) During your pregnancy, pray, asking God for the wisdom to see His career plans for you. Be open to His direction. (2) Give full-time mothering a chance. Don't enter your mothering career with expectations that you won't be fulfilled. If you do, you won't. (3) Practice the mothering styles noted earlier in this book. You may be surprised at how fulfilling mothering can be when God's design for mother-infant attachment is followed. If, after prayer and counsel and at least several months of mothering experience, your decision is to return to your career, then do so considering the next three sections.

Mother Has to Work

There is a story about a fundamentalist who said to a working mother, "You should be home taking care of your child." The mother replied, "We have no home; that's why I'm working." Actually *having* a home and *owning* a home are separate issues. Unfortunately the American dream of owning a home is beyond the reach of many young couples with young children, and a second income may *seem* the answer. Mothers, before you decide to return to work while your child is an infant, consider these points.

Evaluate your priorities. No material possessions are more valuable to your infant than you yourself. Consider whether you can afford not to give your child your full-time self.

What is your worth in dollars and cents to stay at home? Consider exactly what you will have left over by the time you deduct from your paycheck the costs of clothing, food, transportation, child care, increased taxes, and medical bills (children in day-care centers get more infections). You may be surprised at how little you have left over by the time you deduct these expenses.

Plan ahead. Economize and save as much money as you can during the early years of your marriage and during pregnancy, letting the savings from your second income help your family while you are a full-time mother. Saving enough for at least the first three years is wise if possible. Many couples become accustomed to a standard of living that depends on two incomes. Early in your marriage, consider living on one income and saving the other lest you become trapped in the two-income standard of living after the baby arrives.

Consider borrowing the extra income you need until your child is approximately three years old and you can return to work. I don't generally encourage debt, but when it is used to allow a parent to nurture a baby, in my opinion, debt is justified. A common example is when Dad is a student. Our first child, James, was born while I was a "poor intern." Martha juggled mothering and working part-time. We didn't consider alternatives. We could have used her inheritance. Or we could have lowered our standard of living considerably and then borrowed the rest short-term. It is easier to repay money than reparent children. One of the best investments you can make in your child's future is to give him or her the commitment of yourself, at least for the first couple of years and longer if economically possible. Grandparents are often a willing source if they realize that this is probably one of the most valuable investments they can make in their grandchild's future. To illustrate this case, let me share a situation from my own practice. A friend of mine is an investment counselor, and he is always trying to get me into some sound investments. Shortly after the birth of his first grandchild, his daughter mentioned to me that she was planning to return to work within a couple of months because they had become used to a second income and they felt they still needed it. After convincing her of the wisdom of staying home with her child for at least two years and borrowing the extra income, I decided to present this "investment" to her father. I presented the situation to him by saying, "John, I'm calling you about an opportunity for perhaps the best long-term investment you have ever made. Come on down to the office and let's talk about it." After talking to him about his daughter's situation, John agreed that helping care for his grandchild was, indeed, a good investment.

Working at Home

Having a home business may be a realistic answer to the second-income dilemma. Mothers, this works best when you take time to find the type of work you want to do. Doing work that you dislike will wear thin after a while. Some examples of home businesses are caring for children, typing, selling by phone, bookkeeping, sewing, doing arts and crafts, giving piano lessons, and being a sales distributor—jobs in which much of the work is done at home and in which you can take your baby along when you make your calls. Some professional women bring their businesses into their homes and turn their spare rooms into offices. You may be surprised at the variety of work you can do during your baby's times of lower need. I know a mother who is an editor and works on her own portable home computer that is tied into the main office. This mother "goes to the office" without leaving her nest. Another mother has a business of delivering fresh cut flowers that she arranges to homes and offices—her clients love the service and love seeing her baby every week. In her book *The Heart Has Its Own Reasons*, Mary Ann Cahill explores endless possibilities for families who are committed to keeping Mother (or at times, Father) available in the home to nurture the children (see Bibliography).

Working Outside the Home

If having a home business is not possible for you, you may want to consider some other alternatives.

Part-time work. Part-time work has been the greatest change in the working world in the past decade. There is an ever-expanding market for part-time workers because, according to industrial studies, part-time workers offer employers increased efficiency but require fewer financial obligations and fringe benefits. Part-time work is often more attractive to the woman who *wants* to work than it is to the woman who has to work.

A client of mine who switched from full-time to part-time work said, "Full-time work was too much for my baby; full-time at home was too much for me."

Flex-time work. Flex-time is part-time work with flexible hours. Flex-time allows the mother to adjust her hours to be at home when her child is sick or has a special need.

Shared jobs. This type of work arrangement requires the cooperation of two people, each sharing the work of one full-time job. Both parents may share the responsibilities of one job, or two mothers may agree to "cover" for each other when their children have special needs: "I'll work for you if your child is sick, and you'll work for me if my child is sick."

Let's suppose an anxious mother comes to me and says, "I have prayed about this decision and have sought counseling. I have decided that for my personhood and our own family situation, it's best for me to return to my previous career, even though my baby is only three months old. But I want to be a good mother also. I need help." What do I tell her?

I take the Christian approach of offering constructive advice and exploring alternatives instead of imposing destructive guilt. In such cases, I assure mothers that since continuing the attachment relationship is most important, breastfeeding is a positive way to do this.

Efficiency Tips for the Working Mother

If you must work outside the home, the following tips will help you continue your good mothering and indirectly benefit your career.

Plan ahead. Organization is the key to efficient working and mothering. Working outside the home does not allow you much time for cooking and housekeeping. Sit down with your husband and plan menus and chore-sharing so your quality time with your child is not diluted by hours spent on household duties.

You can breastfeed and work. Many mothers would consider breastfeeding and working incompatible. On the contrary, I especially encourage a working mother to breastfeed because this gives her a special tie to her baby and alleviates some of the disappointment of having to leave the baby to go to work.

Some suggestions for breastfeeding while working include:

1. Encourage a long breastfeeding before you go to work, when you return home, and when you put the baby to sleep, depending upon your working

hours. Be available and open to other shorter nursings "on demand" throughout the time you are together. Be prepared for some night nursing.

2. Avoid engorgement. When your breasts feel full, manually or with a pump express your milk to avoid uncomfortable engorgement and a possible breast infection. Store it in a refrigerator or a cooler for the next day's use. You can store your breast milk in an ordinary refrigerator-type freezer for two weeks and in a deep freeze (zero degrees Fahrenheit) for many months. You have a right to request time out from work or a somewhat extended coffee break to pump your milk at least once while at work. Twice is better in terms of having a better milk supply.

3. If you do not work far from home, have your baby-sitter bring your baby to you a couple of times during the day for breastfeeding, or go home at lunchtime for nursing.

4. Some major corporations have day-care centers in the building so that mother and baby can be within nursing distance of each other. You have a right to this time off to express milk or breastfeed. A doctor's prescription can be obtained if necessary; in cases where the employer has objected, the courts have upheld the mother's right to breastfeed her baby while on the job.

5. Expect your baby to nurse several times during the night and more frequently on weekends when you resume full-time mothering. This is a realistic expectation, but you will be understandably tired.

6. Advise your baby-sitter of your expected time of arrival at home, and advise him or her not to feed your baby during the last hour before that time. In this way your baby will eagerly take your breast as soon as you arrive. The first hour after you arrive home should

be a special time of closeness and breastfeeding, a time to be reunited with your infant without any interference from telephones or pressing household chores. Take the phone off the hook, put your feet up, turn some music on, and settle down to nurse your baby. This is also a well-deserved time to unwind from a hard day's work.

Father Feelings and Working Mothers

Fathers, be sensitive to the dilemma facing many of today's mothers. Job satisfaction is equally important to them. It can be difficult for a woman to give up using her hard-earned college degree to stay at home and be a full-time mother. This change of status is especially difficult for the woman who has had an exciting career outside the home before settling into her career inside the home.

It's not easy for a woman to be thought of constantly in reference to somebody else, as somebody's wife or as somebody's mother. What about the woman as a person in relation to herself alone? She isn't really a "self alone" anymore, and neither is her husband. The two became one flesh when they married. They both gave up some of their individual personhood to the relationship.

As a sensitive, caring husband, you should be mindful of these feelings that your wife will probably have at some time during her early adjustment to mothering. Give her positive reinforcement. Convey your consistent love for her as a person, a wife, and a mother. Constantly give her the message that she is doing the most important job in the world: raising another person for Christ.

230

A good example of what not to do is portrayed in the movie *Kramer vs. Kramer.* Prior to having a child, both Mr. and Mrs. Kramer had exciting professional careers. After the birth of their first child, as many professional women do, Mrs. Kramer decided to stay home and devote herself to professional mothering. As Mrs. Kramer became more deeply involved in mothering, Mr. Kramer became less and less involved as a father and more involved in his career. Instead of meeting his wife's emotional needs when he was home, he spent most of his time talking about how exciting his career was. Needless to say, Mrs. Kramer became less and less fulfilled as a person, gave up mothering (and the marriage) entirely, and returned to her career outside the home. Only after Mr. Kramer took over the parenting responsibilities did he realize the daily challenges facing a full-time mother. He learned the real value of the term *homemaker.* This is a classic example of what happens when a husband fails to perform his supporting role in God's design for the family.

If the mother works outside the home, the father works more inside the home. Shared child care is a realistic fact of life, especially if the mother has a job outside the home. The mother also needs some "down time." Nothing in God's order of the family or in the biological makeup of men says men cannot do housework. If the traditional role of the woman is changed somewhat, the traditional role of the man must also change to meet the needs of the entire family.

Father, pitch in and do your share of housework. Help meet your child's daily needs. Actually, one of the fringe benefits of the working mother has been to bring many fathers back into their homes to get them hooked into fathering and into knowing their children better. Father-involvement and shared child care are especially important if your wife continues breastfeeding while working, and I encourage you to encourage her to do just that.

Choosing a Baby-Sitter

One of today's great paradoxes is that at the very time when God's design for mother-infant attachment is becoming more and more realized, the demand for substitute care-giving is increasing. You may be greatly disappointed when you search the marketplace for quality substitute mothering and find that the demand is far greater than the supply. Also, substitute care-giving is just that—a substitute, not a replacement for the mother. The following suggestions discuss different options in child care and how to choose a substitute mother.

Baby-Sitters Are Substitute Mothers

I don't like the term *baby-sitter*. It's too static and unfeeling. Try to find a mother substitute who practices the child-care style you value. Ask leading questions such as, "What do you do when an infant cries?" If you are uncertain about his or her child-care philosophy, say exactly how you want your child mothered in your absence. Be specific: "When he cries, he should be picked up. He should be mothered to sleep. He should be carried around and be in your arms a lot. He should not be left unattended in front of a television set."

Parents, remember, no substitute caregiver has a biological attachment to your child. Don't expect anyone else to have a built-in radar system that intuitively responds to your baby's cues as you do. For this reason you must give your substitute caregiver detailed instruction on how to recognize your baby's cues and how to respond to them. Emphasize the importance of feedback stimulation that is so vital to infant development. When your baby exercises a newly acquired developmental skill, impress upon your caregiver the importance of acknowledging your baby's accomplishments. If no one responds to a developmental skill, a child may be less motivated to exercise that skill. Mothers, spend time together with your baby and the caregiver so he or she can see your mothering modeled.

Use the Same Caregiver

A child who has various baby-sitters will have difficulty forming a love attachment to them. As I have mentioned repeatedly, the ability to form love attachments is one of the major developmental goals of early childhood. Children who are deprived of this consistency may show certain "diseases of nonattachment" that are reflected in aggressive and impulsive or withdrawn behaviors. As your baby learns to talk be prepared for him to call both you and his caregiver "Mama."

Options in Child Care

Toddlers are often more comfortable being cared for in their own homes where they are secure. A one-to-one caregiver-to-child relationship is usually the best for the infant under one year. A rule of thumb is that one caregiver can adequately care for the number of children equal to the number of years, for example, one caregiver per one one year old, two two year olds, three three year olds. The problem with this rule of

233

thumb is that children's needs do not really lessen as they get older, they only change.

If a one-to-one relationship is not economically feasible, try to find a friend with children of a similar age who will care for your child in his or her own home. You also may try the shared child-care arrangement in which a group of three or four working mothers with similar values jointly hire a sitter to come to one of their homes.

Parent-cooperative child care is another alternative. Four or five working mothers with similar values arrange to care for each other's children one day a week. Cared for in a home environment, these children are often of similar ages. This arrangement usually requires that you be licensed by the proper authorities if you care for more than one family's children. Some mothers have opened their homes to care for children as a means of supplementing the family's income; some godly mothers even feel that this is their ministry to children. In most cases, home care is preferable to commercial day-care centers.

Tips on Selecting a Day-Care Center

If a day-care center is the only economically feasible option for your family situation, visit the prospective center and look for the following conditions: (1) What is the ratio of caregivers to children? One caregiver to four infants is the maximum you should accept. (2) Examine the credentials of the staff. Determine if they have special training in cognitive development and have realistic expectations of children at various stages. (3) Are they nurturers? Are they genuinely sensitive to a baby's needs? What do they do when a baby cries? Do they understand the difference between chastisement and punishment? (4) Examine the facilities and the equipment. Are they clean, safe, and designed appropriately for the age and the stage of each child's development?

Parents should look for specific qualities in an infant caregiver. When visiting the facility, watch the prospective caregiver in action and examine his or her nurturing qualities. Does he or she look at, touch, and talk to the child with the message of, "I care, I am interested in you as a person with needs, I am sensitive to you"? Does he or she have a working knowledge of the usual developmental milestones and the realistic expectations of children at various stages? Is he or she resilient and able to adapt to the ever-changing moods of some toddlers? Does he or she have a spontaneous sense of humor? This is a real must for coping with toddlers. Watch how he or she handles a child who has gotten out of control. Is he or she kind but firm? Most importantly, observe how his or her Christian values carry over into his or her child caring. Parents should take their children along to the interview and see how their children relate to the caregiver and vice versa. Children are often the best critics of their own care, but unfortunately they often have no voice in that choice. If a child has a certain sparkle in his or her eyes as he or she relates to the caregiver, parents, you can be sure that there are meaningful waves of communication going between the caregiver and the child. Unfortunately day-care workers have a very high rate of turnover, so the likelihood of having a consistent care-giver is minimal. For this reason alone, day-care centers are inadequate for the child under three.

I am truly sympathetic with mothers who are faced with the dilemma of a dual career. I assure you that we have struggled with this in our own home and have concluded that difficult problems do not have easy solutions. The ideal cannot always be achieved in today's society, but with prayer and support from your Christian community you can try to come close to that ideal.

Bibliography

The following books and reference sources are arranged according to their major subjects, although many of them cover a wide range of topics on parenting. Please bear in mind that when recommending a book, *I am not necessarily endorsing every statement made in it.* I have chosen to recommend those books that, in my opinion, contain important messages that will contribute to your growth as Christian parents. Not all of the books on the following list are specifically Christian, but they are not non-Christian either. I have also chosen those books most in accordance with the philosophy of attachment and feeling right that I have continually advocated in this book.

Abortion

Schaeffer, Francis A. and C. Everett Koop. *Whatever Happened to the Human Race?* Westchester, IL: Crossway, 1983.

> Written by the late renowned Christian philosopher and the former surgeon general of the United States, this book is a real must for understanding the issues surrounding abortion, and it exposes the rapid but subtle loss of human rights.

Swindoll, Charles. *Sanctity of Life: The Inescapable Issue.* Dallas, TX: Word, 1990.

Besides the sanctity of life, Swindoll examines abortion after the fact and makes a plea for morality and the resolve to be strong.

Wilke, Dr. J. C. and Mrs. *Abortion: Questions and Answers*. Cincinnati, OH: Hayes Publishing, 1989.
If you could choose only one book this should be it: a reference manual with questions and answers on all the aspects of abortion.

Breastfeeding

Breastfeeding Organizations. La Leche League International, Inc., 1-800-LA LECHE, P.O. Box 4079, Schaumberg, IL 60168.
This organization not only teaches better mothering through breastfeeding but teaches better mothering in all aspects of parenting and child care. There is a local La Leche League in every major city in the United States and throughout the world. Write for a free catalog of their breastfeeding publications, which contains nearly one hundred books and booklets on all aspects of parenting.

Breastfeeding Your Baby: A Mother's Guide.
A one-hour video produced by Medela, Inc., (the breast pump company) in cooperation with La Leche League. William Sears, M.D., Jay Gordon, M.D., celebrities, and breastfeeding experts instruct and encourage; families speak on breastfeeding's benefits. Available through La Leche League.

Bumgarner, Norma Jane. *Mothering Your Nursing Toddler*. Schaumberg, IL: La Leche League International, Inc., 1982.
Not only does this book extol the virtues of nursing the toddler and not weaning the child before his time, it is a beautiful account of attachment mothering.

Kippley, Sheila. *Breastfeeding and Natural Child Spacing.* The Couple to Couple League International, Inc., P.O. Box 111184, Cincinnati, OH 45211.
> This book discusses the concept of natural mothering and how it can postpone the return of fertility.

Torgus, Judy, ed. *The Womanly Art of Breastfeeding.* Schaumberg, IL: La Leche League International, Inc., 1987.
> The authority for the breastfeeding mother, this book not only deals with the joys and problems of breastfeeding but also affirms the profession of attachment mothering.

Childbirth

Brewer, Gail Sforza and Tom Brewer, M.D. *What Every Pregnant Woman Should Know: The Truth About Diet and Drugs in Pregnancy.* New York: Viking-Penguin, 1985.
> The importance of good nutrition in pregnancy. Relationship of toxemia and diet in pregnancy.

Dick-Read, Grantly. *Childbirth Without Fear.* (5th ed.) Edited by Helen Wessel. New York: Harper and Row, 1984.
> This is a classic book on natural childbirth that demonstrates how laboring women can overcome the fear-tension-pain cycle.

Evans, Debra. *The Complete Book on Childbirth.* Wheaton, IL: Tyndale House, 1986.
> This book is valuable for the original and beautifully expressed concepts on marriage and birth. Her information on breastfeeding is insufficient and I do not completely agree with her attitudes toward pain and childbirth. Readers will want to balance this book with others on Christian childbirth and breastfeeding.

Korte, Diana and Roberta Scaer. *A Good Birth, A Safe Birth.* New York: Bantam, 1990.

239

This basic guide to childbirth options helps expectant parents negotiate to get the kind of birth experience they want. Also provides insight into recent trends in childbirth.

MacNutt, Francis and Judith. *Praying for Your Unborn Child: How Parents' Prayers Can Make a Difference in the Health and Happiness of Their Children.* New York: Doubleday, 1989.
A beautiful and insightful guide to praying for your baby during each stage of pregnancy, from conception to delivery. The authors show how parents who surround their unborn infant with love, prayer, and serenity will profoundly affect their child's personality and well-being.

McCutcheon-Rosegg, Susan and Peter Rosegg. *Natural Childbirth the Bradley Way.* New York: E. P. Dutton-Penguin, 1984.
An updated guide to pregnancy and childbirth. Step-by-step preparations are provided for the couple looking for a totally natural, drug-free birth.

Nilsson, Lennart. *A Child Is Born.* (Rev. ed.) New York: Delacourt, 1990. Also published by Life Education, reprint no. 27. Canaan, NH: Media International.
A series of unprecedented photographs of the development of the embryo, from conception to birth, the book will help you realize the true miracle of fetal development and how a Supreme Architect is certainly in charge of this development.

Noble, Elizabeth. *Having Twins: A Parent's Guide to Pregnancy, Birth and Early Childhood.* Boston, MA: Houghton-Mifflin, 1991.
A veteran childbirth expert tells how to carry healthy babies to term.

Odent, Michael, M.D. *Birth Reborn.* New York: Random House, 1984.

A beautifully illustrated description of birth at Pithiviers in France, using explicit photography to help demonstrate how birth is best achieved in the modified (standing) squat position and also with the aid of tubs. The description of how birth can be a normal, safe, and confident part of life encourages couples in planning the birth they want.

Sears, William M. and Linda H. Holt. *The Pregnancy Book: A Month-by-Month Guide.* New York: Little Brown Co., 1997.

Wessel, Helen. *Natural Childbirth and the Christian Family.* Bookmates International, Inc., Apple Tree Family Ministries, P.O. Box 2083, Artesia, CA 90702–2083, 562-925-0149.

A must for all parents who are taking prepared-childbirth classes. Mrs. Wessel, a mother of six, adds a Christian perspective to the childbirth-without-fear techniques described by Dr. Grantly Dick-Read.

_____. *Under the Apple Tree.* Fresno, CA: Bookmates International, Inc., 1982. (See above for address to write for booklet.)

An absolute must for Christian parents-to-be. Mrs. Wessel discusses the scriptural basis of marriage, birthing, and early parenting practices; it should be read and studied by husband and wife together.

Discipline

Craig, Sydney. *Raising Your Child Not by Force but by Love.* Philadelphia, PA: The Westminster Press, 1973.

This book, written from a Christian perspective, helps parents gain an understanding of discipline as a *positive* concept. It has great insight into the feelings of children and the effect of our discipline (good and bad) on their feelings. It also gives insight into why we get angry with our children and alternative ways of expressing and managing anger.

BIBLIOGRAPHY

Crary, Elizabeth. *Without Spanking or Spoiling*. Seattle, WA: Parenting Press, 1979.
Alternatives for parents to recognize and attain their personal goals in childrearing.

_____. *Kids Can Cooperate: A Practical Guide to Teaching Problem Solving*. Seattle, WA: Parenting Press, 1984.
Teaches children skills to solve conflicts themselves.

_____. *Pick Up Your Socks . . . And Other Skills Growing Children Need*. Seattle, WA: Parenting Press, 1990.
Teaches children responsibility skills.

Faber, Adele and Elaine Mazlish. *Siblings Without Rivalry*. New York: Avon, 1987.
Help your children live together so you can live too.

_____. *How to Talk So Kids Will Listen and Listen So Kids Will Talk*. New York: Avon, 1982.
Communication skills for parents: how to listen and deal with feelings; alternatives to nagging and punishment.

Fennema, Jack. *Nurturing Children in the Lord*. Phillipsburg, NJ: Presbyterian and Reformed Publishing, 1977.
A study guide on developing a biblical approach to discipline, this is an excellent book for Christian parents who wish to base their discipline on scriptural principles.

Kesler, Jay. *Too Big to Spank*. Ventura, CA: Regal, 1978.
This is a practical guide for parents to help them discipline and build self-esteem in their teenager.

Leman, Kevin. *Making Children Mind Without Losing Yours*. Old Tappan, NJ: Revell, 1984.
Should have been titled *Helping Children Mind* by Dr. Leman's own admission. A practical, commonsense approach to discipline based on action (but rarely spanking), not words. Called Reality Discipline, it teaches children to be accountable for their actions.

Only one area of concern: Dr. Leman advises parents to leave their young babies at home so they can get out now and then. I encourage couples to get out together and take baby too.

Narramore, S. Bruce. *Help! I'm a Parent*. Grand Rapids, MI: Zondervan, 1972.
This book applies both psychological and biblical principles in arriving at a systematic approach to discipline.

Sears, William M. and Martha Sears. *The Discipline Book: Everything You Need to Know to Have a Better Behaved Child*. New York: Little Brown Co., 1995.

Stewart, Blaize Clement. *The Loving Parent: A Guide to Growing Up Before Your Children Do*. San Luis Obispo, CA: Impact, 1988.
A secular book dealing sensitively with issues such as obedience, lying, stealing, cheating, anger, and sexuality.

Divorce

Hart, Archibald D. *Children and Divorce—What to Expect, How to Help*. Waco, TX: Word, 1982.
Written by a Christian psychologist, this realistic and helpful guidebook helps divorcing parents understand their children's feelings and help them cope.

Smith, Virginia Watts. *The Single Parent*. Old Tappan, NJ: Revell, 1979.
This very sensitive Christian guide to the plight of the single parent offers sympathetic understanding and practical advice on the dilemma of achieving personal fulfillment and rearing a child for Christ.

Education

Elkind, David. *The Hurried Child, Growing Up Too Fast, Too Soon*. Reading, MA: Addison-Wesley, 1989.

Offers insight and advice on the burden of stress on modern children who are "forced to bloom."

Harris, Gregg. *The Christian Home School.* Brentwood, TN: Wolgemuth & Hyatt, 1987.
A good starter book for families considering home school.

Macauley, Susan Schaeffer. *For the Children's Sake: Foundations of Education for Home and School.* Westchester, IL: Crossway, 1987.
The daughter of the late Christian philosopher Francis A. Schaeffer, who grew up in Switzerland and L'Abri Fellowship, writes about the wonderful, life-enriching, joyous experience education can be for your child, in your home and in school.

Montessori, Maria. *The Discovery of the Child.* New York: Ballantine, 1967.
A good explanation of the Montessori philosophy of education, this book defines the needs and offers practical education suggestions for the various sensitive periods of the child.

Moore, Raymond S. and Dorothy N. *Home Grown Kids.* Waco, TX: Word, 1981.
A practical handbook for teaching your children at home, this book calls attention to the fact that education is still the prime responsibility of the parent. The educational suggestions are provocative and well worth considering; however, I do not agree with some of the authors' suggestions on early child care, especially much of their nutritional advice.

Sears, William M. and L. Thompson. *The A.D.D. Book: Attention Deficit Disorder.* New York: Little Brown Co., 1998.

Uphoff, James K., June E. Gilmore, and Rosemarie Huber. *Summer Children—Ready or Not for School.* J & J

Publishing Co., P.O. Box 8549, Middletown, OH 45042.

Marriage

Crabb, Lawrence Jr. *How to Become One with Your Mate*. Grand Rapids, MI: Zondervan, 1982.
> This is a small, very readable excerpt from *The Marriage Builder*, by Lawrence Crabb, on oneness of body and spirit in the marriage relationship. Looking to Christ to fulfill our needs enables us to minister to our mates.

Harley, Willard. *His Needs, Her Needs: Building an Affair-Proof Marriage*. Old Tappan, NJ: Revell, 1986.
> Identifies the ten most important marital needs of husbands and wives and teaches how those needs can be fulfilled.

Wheat, Ed, M.D. and Gloria Okes Perkins. *Love Life for Every Married Couple*. Grand Rapids, MI: Zondervan, 1980.
> How to fall in love, stay in love, rekindle your love.

Media

Farah, Joseph (editor). *Between the Lines*. 325 Pennsylvania Ave., SE, Washington, DC 20003.
> A biweekly newsletter covering the politics and morality of the news media and entertainment industry.

Lappe, Francis Moore. *What to Do After You Turn Off the TV*. New York: Ballantine, 1985.

For other information concerning media write:

> Christian Leaders for Responsible Television
> c/o American Family Association
> P.O. Box 2440
> Tupelo, MS 38803

BIBLIOGRAPHY

Mother-Infant Attachment

Fraiberg, Selma. "Every Child's Birthright." In *Selected Writings of Selma Fraiberg*. Louis Fraiberg, editor. Columbus, OH: Ohio State University Press, 1987.

Kaplan, Louise. *Oneness and Separateness: From Infant to Individual*. New York: Simon and Schuster, 1978.
  A beautiful discussion of the inner workings of the child as he goes from oneness to separateness. Dr. Kaplan explores some of the theory of the benefits of mother-infant attachment and the consequences of premature detachment.

Klaus and Kennell. *Parent-Infant Bonding*. Saint Louis, MO: C. V. Mosby, 1982.
  This book discusses results of studies that suggest the positive benefits of mother and baby remaining in close contact with each other immediately after birth.

McClure, Vimala Schneider. *Infant Massage*. New York: Bantam, 1989.
  Teaches parents to discover the joys and benefits of massage for their babies and for themselves. Photographs illustrate each step of the process. Massage promotes bonding, reduces tension and fussing, and aids in physical development. I highly recommend this book.

Montagu, Ashley. *Touching: The Human Significance of the Skin*. New York: Harper and Row, 1986.
  The classical treatise on the importance of the skin as the largest organ of human sensation. Dr. Montagu discusses at length the psychological benefits of skin-to-skin contact.

Natural Family Planning

Kass-Annese, Barbara, R.N., N.P., and Hal Danzer, M.D. *The Fertility Awareness Workbook*. New York: Putnam, 1981.

A concise, how-to book on natural family planning. Good illustrations and diagrams.

Kippley, Sheila. *Breastfeeding and Natural Child Spacing*. Cincinnati, OH: The Couple to Couple League International, Inc., 1989.

This book discusses the concept of natural mothering and how it can postpone the return of fertility.

Kippley, John and Sheila. *The Art of Natural Family Planning*. Cincinnati, OH: The Couple to Couple League International, Inc., 1989.

To be used either on your own or as part of an instructional program, the book teaches the sympto-thermal method of fertility control. Part One explains the "why" of NFP; Part Two the "how to." My favorite chapter is entitled "Marriage Building with NFP."

New Age

Kjos, Barit. *Your Child and the New Age*. Wheaton, IL: Victor, 1990.

A solid explanation of various aspects of the New Age influence in schools and media, with practical suggestions on what parents can do. Issues such as counterfeit spirituality, values clarification, New Age globalism in schools, mind manipulation, distortion of imagination, pagan sentiments in toys, TV, movies, reading material, and music.

Michaelsen, Johanna. *Like Lambs to the Slaughter: Your Child and the Occult*. Eugene, OR: Harvest House, 1989.

Information parents need to have to help their children survive or avoid the subtle and not-so-subtle New Age influences in the world today.

Parenting and Child Care

Cahill, Mary Ann. *The Heart Has Its Own Reasons*. New York: New American Library, 1985.

This book encourages mothers to stay home with their children and gives practical and timely suggestions on how that can be managed financially.

Campbell, D. Ross. *How to Really Love Your Child*. Wheaton, IL: Victor, 1978.
This book, written by a Christian psychiatrist, discusses the importance of touching, eye-to-eye contact, and focused attention. It offers practical tips on how to convey your love to your child.

_____. *How to Really Love Your Teenager*. Wheaton, IL: Victor, 1981.
Encouraging guidance for parents struggling to understand and express love to their teens. Picks up where *How to Really Love Your Child* leaves off.

Crook, William G. and Laura J. Stevens. *Solving the Puzzle of Your Hard to Raise Child*. New York: Random House, 1987.
Parents of high-need children need the information in this book concerning the effect on behavior of improper or inadequate nutrition. Tells how to improve the child's diet and, therefore, his behavior.

Dobson, James. *Hide or Seek*. Tappan, NJ: Revell, 1979.
In my opinion this is the best of Dr. Dobson's many books. It deals with the extremely important issue of how to build self-esteem in your child.

_____. *Preparing for Adolescence*. New York: Bantam, 1980.
An excellent text for parent and preteen to share, with an accompanying study guide for your child. I've used it as each of our first four approached their teen years.

Noble, Elizabeth. *Having Twins: A Parent's Guide to Pregnancy, Birth, and Early Childhood*. Boston, MA: Houghton-Mifflin, 1991.

A veteran childbirth expert tells how to carry healthy babies to term.

Sears, William M. and Martha Sears. *The Baby Book: Everything You Need to Know About Your Baby—From Birth to Age Two*. New York: Little Brown Co., 1993.

_____. *Becoming a Father: How to Nurture and Enjoy Your Family*. Schaumberg, IL: La Leche League International, 1986.

_____. *Growing Together: A Parents' Guide to Baby's First Year*. Schaumberg, IL: La Leche League International, 1987.
This book describes the month-by-month development of babies from birth to one year.

_____. *Nighttime Parenting*. Schaumberg, IL: La Leche League International, 1987.
Practical tips for parenting your child to sleep.

_____. *Parenting the Fussy Baby and High Need Child*. New York: Little Brown Co., 1996.

_____. *SIDS: A Parent's Guide to Understanding and Preventing the Sudden Infant Death Syndrome*. New York: Little Brown Co., 1995.

Sex Education

Andry, Andrew and Stephen Schepp. *How Babies Are Made*. New York: Little-Brown, 1984.
This is the perfect starter book for teaching the reproductive process to your children. Illustrated with paper sculpture, figures are realistic and simple. Begins with plants and animals, and tastefully illustrates humans, for ages 3–10. Ends with the mother breastfeeding her baby.

Kitzinger, Sheila and Lennart Nilsson. *Being Born*. New York: Grosset Dunlap, 1986.

The same magnificent photos of Nilssons's *A Child Is Born* combined with poetic text about conception and birth make this book timeless. Adults as well as children are drawn to it, even though it is written for children.

McDowell, Josh and Dick Day. *Why Wait? What You Need to Know About the Teen Sexuality Crisis*. San Bernardino, CA: Here's Life Publishers, 1987.

A very frank look at the situation challenging teens and the biblical perspective on what God wants for their lives in regard to chastity.

Sexuality

Evans, Debra. *The Mystery of Womanhood*. Westchester, IL: Crossway, 1987.

A biblical perspective on being a woman, finding the inner beauty of femininity, handling stress of daily living, fertility and childbearing, sexuality in a healthy marriage, and living with a cyclical nature.

Penner, Clifford and Joyce. *The Gift of Sex: A Christian Guide to Sexual Fulfillment*. Waco, TX: Word, 1981.

A comprehensive and joyful guide to sex for Christians.

Sleep Problems

Sears, William. *Nighttime Parenting*. Schaumberg, IL: La Leche League International, 1987.

Practical tips for parenting your child to sleep.

Thevenin, Tine. *The Family Bed*. New York: Avery, 1987.

This book brings back an age-old concept in child rearing and advocates children sleeping with their parents or with other siblings as a way to solve bedtime problems, create a closer bond within the family, and give children a greater sense of security.

Your Child's Devotional Life

Blitchington, Evelyn. *The Family Devotions Idea Book*. Minneapolis, MN: Bethany House, 1982.
    This book is full of practical ideas on how to conduct meaningful family devotions.

Chapin, Alice. *Building Your Child's Faith*. Nashville, TN: Thomas Nelson, 1990.
    Simple, fun ideas for teaching children how to pray, worship, and discover the Bible.

Haystead, Wes. *Teaching Your Child About God*. Ventura, CA: Regal, 1981.
    This is an easy-to-read book with practical advice on the spiritual training of the child at various stages.

Index

abdominal pain, 107, 108, 109
  see also colic
acetaminophen, 126, 127–29, 141, 162
allergies, 65, 88, 89, 93, 94, 96, 103, 106, 107–10, 134, 136, 139, 142, 152, 202–3
  common allergens, 109–10, 202, 203
  prevention of, 110
  symptoms of, 108, 109, 202
anemia, 89, 107
anger, 15, 42, 59, 88
antibiotics, 126, 136–37, 139–40, 142–43, 144, 166
aspirin, 127, 130–31, 141, 162
attachment parenting, xii, xiii, xiv, iv, 5–11, 14–18, 19–23, 24, 25, 26, 35, 38, 50,

66, 71, 76–77, 169, 210, 217–18
baby-sitters, 232–34
babysling, 46, 48, 55, 60
baby swing, 60
babywearing, xii, 12, 46–48
balance, xiii, 12, 13–14
bedsharing, xiii, 12, 159, 178–80, 181–93, 204, 209
  and sexual relations, 185–86, 210
birthmarks, 118
bonding, xii, 12, 13, 25, 47
boundaries, xiii, 12
bowel movements, 97–98
breastfeeding, xii, xiv, 11, 12, 53, 61, 83, 85, 88, 89, 90, 92, 101, 106, 108, 110, 139, 145, 146, 153, 157, 182, 183, 196, 201 202, 208, 209, 211, 228, 229–30
  see also nursing

About the Authors

William Sears, M.D., and his wife, Martha Sears, R.N., have more than two decades of professional pediatric experience. Dr. Sears is clinical assistant professor of pediatrics at the University of Southern California School of Medicine and a practicing pediatrician. Martha Sears is a registered nurse and a certified childbirth educator.

They have cared for more than ten thousand babies, including eight of their own. Dr. Sears has written twelve books on raising children, including five with his wife.

LOOK FOR THESE OTHER BOOKS IN THE SEARS PARENTING LIBRARY

So You're Going To Be A Parent
Practical advice for the soon-to-be mom and dad. Provides information on healthy living during pregnancy, as well as what to expect during and after the delivery.

0-7852-7206-2 • 216 pages • Mass Market Paperback

The Growing Years
Expert advice on the ins and outs of raising your child. Includes tips on discipline, toilet training, choosing schools, and more. Also includes a section for single parents.

0-7852-7208-9 • 300 pages • Mass Market Paperback